T O BE WHAT
WE ARE, AND TO
BECOME WHAT WE
ARE CAPABLE OF
BECOMING, IS THE
ONLY END OF LIFE.

—ROBERT LOUIS STEVENSON

LOOK AT IT THIS WAY

by

DON SPATZ

and

A. AUBREY BODINE

Published by

Bodine & Associates, Inc.
Baltimore, Maryland

1975

Second Edition
Library of Congress Catalog No. 75-13122
SBN 910254-08-7
Copyright 1975 by Bodine & Associates, Inc.
Printed in the U.S.A.

Foreword

I was delighted when the publisher suggested illustrating this book with pictures by A. Aubrey Bodine, whose beautiful photography I have admired for many, many years.

None of my material was written expressly to "fit" the accompanying photographs, for we have both explored related areas of the human experience; Mr. Bodine with his camera, and I through my radio commentaries. The task, then, reduced itself to seeking compatible expressions of common interest, which meant pleasant hours combing the artist's massive files and wading through my own mountain of accumulated scripts. Such subsequent revision as I then undertook was necessitated by the fact that writing for the ear is one thing, for the eye, another.

I had the pleasure of meeting Mr. Bodine just once. A number of years ago I interviewed him for a radio broadcast, and it was a memorable experience. He was an extraordinary individual. I recall a statement he made when I asked what motivated him as he trained his lens on a particular subject. What did he look for? "Beauty, mainly," was his reply, adding after a reflective pause: "But remember, beauty occurs in many forms."

You will, most surely, be aware of the Bodine concept of beauty as you peruse the volume you now hold in your hands. I can only hope you will find my accompanying text appropriate. I certainly consider that I am in excellent company.

DON SPATZ

Introduction

It is 7:35 a.m. on any given weekday, and people in five states are listening to WBAL Radio in Baltimore. The news is winding down; the announcer signs off. The next voice you hear is that of Don Spatz. Following a broadcast, if the pattern holds, as many as fifty people might sit down to write a letter to Spatz. His few minutes on the air each day move listeners to respond with 25,000 letters a year. Who is Don Spatz, and why do so many write him?

Don Spatz is a former radio drama writer, music critic, and public relations director for the Peabody Conservatory of Music. Over ten years ago, WBAL began broadcasting his daily five-minute program of personal anecdotes and commentary, and the program has been growing in popularity ever since. This book is a collection of many of his favorite pieces. Most are illustrated by a Bodine picture.

His listeners write because Don Spatz sifts through the variety of human experiences and picks out moments of heroism. In a world in which events often reflect uncharitable and arrogant behavior, he finds and writes about the simple acts of unselfishness and humility he finds in daily life. His writing reflects an unbounded optimism founded on the certainty that if there is anything human beings have in common, anything that can unite them, it is the noble instincts revealed in the heroism of people—all people.

Spatz tells us that it is character—which he defines as "what you are when nobody is looking"—that makes all men kin, ordinary people and the great and powerful too. His heroes include the mailman who turned the dusty road bed into a garden by planting flower seeds along his route every day, the truckdriver who volunteered his services one day each week to destitute farmers, the boxer who prayed before each fight that no one would be hurt. He likes to tell the story of the young stranger who stopped to help a poor black man struggling with a heavy load on a cold winter's day; the stranger turned out to be Theodore Roosevelt, the black man Booker T. Washington. He describes the courage and humility that enabled Madame Curie to overcome poverty and personal disaster and Richard Byrd to conquer the South Pole. Character, Spatz would have it, makes all men kin.

A favorite Spatz technique is to describe two people of diverse backgrounds and personalities, and then to bring them together in a situation that shows what they share as human beings. That the talents of Donald Spatz and A. Aubrey Bodine—the Baltimore *Sunpapers'* internationally-known photographer who died in 1970—have been combined to create this book is the kind of story Spatz himself would delight in telling.

Here is Spatz, sophisticated, urbane and optimistic, using his rich vocabulary to describe noble deeds where he finds them. Then, there is Bodine, crusty, cynical and salty, his personality characterized by a legendary cantankerousness.

Yet this book dramatizes what each of these remarkable men do have in common: the view that their role as artists lies in celebrating what is majestic in nature and human experience. Spatz likes to write of man's finer moments; Bodine would not take a picture that wasn't a compliment to its subject—person, place or thing. It is not by accident that Bodine's photography complements Spatz's writing so effectively. Thus, this book is an ingenious bringing together of inspirational writing and sensitive photographs that fit one with the other as if both men had planned it that way.

Despite their different personalities, Spatz and Bodine share a special point of view. Which is why this collection of their work is so aptly titled, *Look at it This Way. This Way* is their way—for all of us, an inspiring one.

GILBERT SANDLER

Bridges

B ridges have always held a strange fascination for me. Their nearness to water has something to do with it, and so does the inherent grace I find in even the smallest, most ancient and severely broken-down specimen. But most importantly, it is the symbolic status that they occupy, for me, in the human condition.

In a religious publication, I one time read an interesting article about bridges. Both kinds. Bridges of steel of stone or wood, that connect two geographical points, and bridges we erect between ourselves and others by the way we live, by what we do, by what we are. These are two different varieties, to be sure, but they serve vital and similar functions.

As we need bridges in order that we may go to land areas that would otherwise be inaccessible, or that we would have to travel to by roundabout routes, so do we need bridges of understanding, friendship, brotherhood, to strengthen our links with those who together with us make up our world. Of the latter, there are many: the bridges between parent and child, between one generation and another, between strangers, between nations. And as with the bridges that connect one shore of a stream with the other, these too require constant attention and upkeep. Only by repair and reconstruction can they be kept in working order.

A bridge, well attended, may stand a long time. Ignored, it can collapse swiftly in decay.

Now I realize there are many stories that illustrate the kind of care I'm talking about. We seldom find them in prominent positions in newspapers, rarely do they occupy lead spots in the news on broadcast media, but they are in constant supply. Let me mention just one that was released as I was preparing the copy for this volume.

It concerned a man just into middle age who put a classified ad in his town's newspaper offering his services one day a week, without charge, to any farmer in the vicinity who needed help in caring for his land and crops. He selected the poorest, most destitute of the many who responded, and one day each week he goes to that farm and works from dawn to dusk doing whatever the owner asks of him. In speaking of it, he says that he gets good exercise, but more importantly, he is extending himself in the service of another.

The man is a truck driver, but he is also a builder of bridges. He has built a most magnificent span between himself and his fellows, a span of faith and understanding and love. We need as many bridges of this sort as we can get. They are not made of steel or concrete, on pilings that sink deep into the soil, with arches that grace the sky above, but they too are strong and they do a great service for those who travel on their lanes.

What's more, they encourage two-way traffic.

The bird that sings

Faith, in the words of Rabindranath Tagore, is the bird that sings when the dawn is still dark. How beautiful and how comforting those words are!

I thought of them as I listened to a radio sermon broadcast by a noted minister, who stated that the deterioration of government begins when decay destroys the principles on which it is founded. In itself, a statement of no great profundity, but one that assumes wider meaning when you apply it to all institutions and endeavor, not just government. When principles rot the structure they support collapses. And you need no sharp eyes to see such degeneration on all fronts these days.

When this happens, we are forced to re-study our values, our beliefs, our standards. And we need to rekindle the flame of faith!

As China becomes a more open society, accessible to the rest of the world, we are learning much about this monolithic land. A traveler to the Peoples' Republic of China, Michael Gill, wrote for a British publication of some of the almost unbelievable accomplishments there. Fully aware that life is severely restricted, he nevertheless noted that police are hardly visible except occasionally to direct traffic. There is no need to lock one's doors because private possessions are safe, and drug addiction, prostitution and alcoholism have been virtually eliminated. Mr. Gill further observed that pleasure, satisfaction, success, progress, even happiness, are measured in small, personal terms, in acts as simple as the contemplation of a budding flower. Mr. Gill wrote of watching his interpreter in Peking, a man of middle age, who stood stock still for half an hour, savoring the beauty of the sunset along the shore of a lake.

I mention this writer and his comments on life in a Communist country because, when traditions tumble, when old established principles are weakened and faith wobbles, we must turn to eternals for sustenance. Where else?

Faith! Has yours been threatened? Have you looked about you and found it growing faint?

There is cause for despair, to be sure. But there is cause for hope, too. The bird that sings when the dawn is still dark, has faith that light will follow.

Read carefully, please, these lines from one of the most remarkable documents on faith ever written: "The best remedy for those who are afraid, lonely or unhappy, is to go outside, somewhere where they can be quite alone with the heavens, with nature and God. Because only then does one feel that all is as it should be and that God wishes to see people happy. As long as this exists, I know there will always be comfort for every sorrow, whatever the circumstances may be."

Those lines are drawn from the diary of the very young Anne Frank.

One small candle

They sat together in the circular room. They were old friends, these two, and there was much talking, for they had not seen each other in many years.

They had come from the same small town, had gone to school together as boys, and then their paths had parted. Frank had moved away, out into the world; he had known success, he had met good fortune, he had even achieved a measure of fame. It was obvious that the fates had been generous, in the way he dressed, the way he talked, the way he behaved.

Tom had stayed home. He had remained in the town where he was born and had lived a comfortable, but not exciting, life. And then in his later years, he had moved to a barren clump of rocks just off the coast—and on a clear day, he could see the mainland, to the very house in which he had spent so many years of his life. And when his wife died, he stayed on, living on the island, doing his job in his own quiet and efficient way.

Now they were together.

Frank had come for a visit, and they reminisced, chatting about the old days, probing their memories for the mutual experiences that old friends share. Outside, there was the constant roar of the sea, crashing on the rocks, and above this the rising moan of the wind. There was a storm brewing, without doubt, and it would be a bad one. They would have to tie up the small boat in which Frank had come from shore, and Frank would have to spend the night on the island.

Inside, where they sat, it was warm and cozy, and over a glass of sherry the talk continued to flow. And despite his best effort, Frank found himself being just a trifle superior. It crept into his words, though he didn't want it to. But then, he had been the one who ventured out into the world, he had been the one to give his name a bit of luster.

And then, the first fingers of twilight entered the room, and Tom went to a cabinet and took out a candle. With a match, he lit it, and the flickering flame sent shadows dancing on the walls. Tom went to a door that opened onto the first step of the winding, circular stairs, and he asked Frank if he wanted to go along.

"Where?"

"Up, high above the room where you will sleep tonight." And together they climbed to the uppermost level of the lighthouse. "This is the entrance to the harbor. As the ships approach, they look to me for the light to guide them safely through the channel." Tom held the flickering candle, and Frank, looking at it, said: "With *that* you light the way?"

Tom moved around to the huge lamps that stood near the windows with their great, polished reflectors. With his candle, he brought them one by one to flaming brilliance. "In the storm, they'll need me tonight, more than ever. They'll look for the light from this one small candle."

H*arry Fleischman is the Race Relations Coordinator of the American Jewish Committee. He has a daughter, Martha. When she was in second grade, her teacher asked the children what their fathers did for a living. For most of the youngsters, it was easy: My daddy's a letter carrier, he brings people mail. My father's a fireman, he saves people. My pop's a carpenter, he nails things. And so on. When it came Martha's turn, she hesitated briefly, then said: "My Daddy helps people to be friends with each other."*

What a marvelous occupation!

First person singular

O*ne time* while on a motor trip through New England, I was privileged to meet the great French-born symphony orchestra conductor, Pierre Monteux. This was in Maine, where he directed a school and lived as frequently as his international obligations permitted.

M. Monteux was a short, squat man who wore an enormous moustache that made him rather resemble a benign walrus, but he was a giant to me. And I am not referring to his musicianship or his ability as a conductor, which were monumental. I am referring to Pierre Monteux, the human being.

You see, the veteran conductor and his wife, together with their French poodle, spent part of a summer holiday just as I was doing, rambling from one beauty spot to another in New England. One late afternoon in Massachusetts they decided to seek a motel to spend the night, and upon spotting one that appealed to them, they went into the office to speak to the manager. She told them, somewhat curtly, there were no vacancies. But a young man standing nearby recognized Monteux, hurriedly whispered something to the manager, and the woman's attitude changed immediately. "I believe I do have a vacancy after all," she said. "You see, I didn't realize you were somebody." And Pierre Monteux froze. He bowed stiffly to the motel manager and said: "Madame, everybody is somebody." He and his wife found another place to spend the night.

Humility!

Were we all to possess such wisdom, what giants we would be. Instead, sometimes, some of us, set ourselves up as judges, as arbiters. We presume the awesome power to draw a line between ourselves and others, we determine that we are superior, we elevate ourselves to a plateau more lofty than that of our brothers. And we back our arrogance with clever reasoning, with what we sometimes label scientific proof, we even call it logic. And in so doing, we make of ourselves not giants, but pygmies.

Does anyone remember a man named Sidney Walker? Perhaps it would be more helpful to give you the name by which he was better known—Beau Jack.

Beau Jack was a man of true humility. And greatness! Mark you, *greatness*! He was an illiterate from Augusta, Georgia, who made his name known in his day when he earned the New York State title as lightweight champion of the world. But it is not for his achievements as a fighter that I tip my hat in his memory. No, one time a reporter interviewed him in his dressing room and asked if it was true that he prayed before every fight. Beau Jack admitted that he did. "I pray that nobody get hurt. Then I pray it be a good fight." His visitor asked: "Don't you ever pray to win?" "No," said Beau Jack. "Suppose I pray to win? The other boy, he pray to win too. Then what is God going to do?"

Be it ever so humble

In a doctor's waiting room, I picked up an old magazine and read of a soldier, his wife and children, who lived for a time in a hotel near the Army base where the service man was stationed. One day the youngest child—a girl—was "playing house" in the lobby, when a guest, watching her, said: "It's too bad, my dear, that you don't have a home." "Oh, we have a home," said the child. "We just don't have a house to put it in."

A warm, delightful episode, and it made me think of places that I have passed while driving in the country.

One, some miles from the city, is a little piece of farm property with a battered, dilapidated house that stands close to the highway, a house that may at one time in the distant past have known a coat of paint. Falling down, now, this hovel exudes poverty. But there are always bright, cheerful flowers at the windows, and there are toys on the porch, and the wash (when I see it hanging on the line) is clean. There are children of various ages, playing, happy. The little dog always appears to be sharing their pleasures with them.

I have often wished that I could stop, go inside, meet the family that lives there. I am certain there is warmth and joy and love in that family. You can sense it. You can "feel" it driving by. Those who live in that ramshackle heap would, I know, be branded "underprivileged" by today's standards, but in a far more important measure, I suspect, I am sure, they are greatly privileged!

"A real home," someone has written, "is a shelter from the storms of life, a place of peace and rest. A true home is the center of all human hopes and dreams, and it needs not be a mansion."

There is another house that I remember . . .

Making regular visits to Pennsylvania, I passed it frequently. Small, white, tidy. Flowers in profusion every spring, neatly tended lawn, fruit trees nearby. Obviously a happy family lived there, too. Then one day I drove by and there was a great crowd around the house, strings of cars parked along the road. Auction! Signs indicated that the house and everything in it were up for sale. What happened? I never knew. But I still pass that place, now and again, and it is deserted. . . Empty! Fallen to decay.

There is something ineffably sad about a dwelling when its occupants have gone away. It marks the close of a chapter, the end of something warm and precious. Where once there was a family and children and pets and laughter and song and love—there is now the dreadful sound of silence. Bare walls, dust, echoes, spiders' webs, decay.

There are times, driving by, when I turn my head and look the other way.

The ghost ship

History tells us it was Roald Amundsen, the Norwegian explorer, who in 1906 successfully navigated the Northwest Passage, connecting the Pacific and Atlantic oceans for the first time.

A slight error. He was not the first.

On the morning of August 12, 1775, the whaleship *Herald* out of Greenland, was picking her way through treacherous icebergs when the lookout suddenly spied the masts of a schooner approaching some three miles distant. The *Herald's* Captain Warren with his telescope saw that her sails hung in tatters, her spars and rigging were coated with ice. Closer, they saw no sign of life on board, and when it was possible, they lowered a longboat to investigate. The schooner's name was *Octavius*.

Captain Warren's crew was fearful and suspicious, nevertheless they went aboard the creaking, rotting vessel. The deck was slippery with ice and snow. Finding no one topside, they went below, where, to their horror, they found twenty-eight crewmen frozen in death.

In the *Octavius's* captain's cabin they found the master himself, frozen at his desk. Nearby, a woman, three more men of the crew, and a child. There was a man in the corner, his hands still gripping a flint and a piece of steel.

Captain Warren's crew caused such a fuss, insisting that they leave the ghostly ship at once, so Captain Warren took the logbook from the *Octavius* and returned to his own vessel. Once there they saw the ghostly vessel drift slowly away, never to be seen again on the face of the earth.

It was then the depth of the mystery became apparent.

When Warren studied the log, he found that the *Octavius* had sailed from England, bound for China, *fourteen years before!* The last page of the log, dated November 11, 1762, read: "We have now been enclosed in ice seventeen days. Our last position, Longitude 160 W, Latitude 75 N. The fire went out yesterday and the mate is trying to rekindle it with flint and steel but without success. The master's son died this morning, his wife says she no longer feels the cold."

Incredibly, the *Octavius*, on the day of the last entry in the log, had been ice-bound north of Point Barrow, Alaska, and had since, with all on board frozen to death, drifted thousands of miles, for years, with no hand at the helm, through the treacherous Northwest Passage. She had started in the Pacific, and inch by inch, had drifted eastward, withstanding the constant fury of the elements, to the Atlantic.

The *Octavius*, all on board frozen for thirteen years, was the first vessel to navigate the legendary Northwest Passage.

More nuts than timber

The census taker was making his rounds, and he stopped at a fairly large house in the middle of the block. Of the woman who responded to his knock, he asked many questions, including: "How many children do you have?"

"Let me see," she mused. "There's Ruby and Sarah and Billy and Tom—"

"Never mind the names. Just give me the number."

"They don't have numbers. They all have names!"

Ah, yes, we all have names. And there are some people who never let you forget it. Through no design of their own they possess a distinguished ancestry, and they constantly bask in the reflected glory of that lineage, conveniently forgetting that some family trees produce more nuts than timber. They wave that name of theirs under other's noses as if it really represented something. For them, I gleefully resurrect a story attributed to Will Rogers.

You remember, I'm sure, that Rogers was part-Indian. American Indian. One time he met a man who snootily informed him that he carried a proud name and that his ancestors had come to this country on the Mayflower. "What about yours, Mr. Rogers?"

"Mine," said Will, "met the boat."

This subject never fails to remind me of one of the truly luminous names in American history. Abraham Lincoln. Remember what he said? "I am less concerned about my ancestry than I am over what kind of ancestor I will be."

A name means nothing until *you* endow it with value. It's given to you. You acquire it before you know what a name is. You don't work for it. There is no purchase price. The trick is to give it meaning, a luster of its own. Shakespeare asked what's in a name, and the answer is: Nothing. Nothing until its owner gives it substance.

Who were Michaelangelos parents?

Leonardo da Vinci's grandparents?

Galileo's aunts?

Who cares?

Take your name. It may be common, with hundreds like it in the telephone directory. Smith, for example. You can make it stand out. You can make it unique. It's yours, and you have the power. *You* can be a noble ancestor. Now *that* can mean something.

If you feel as I do and you ever get involved in an argument, as I have, over the value of a name, there's an old Chinese proverb that may silence the opposition. "If you boast only of your ancestors, you admit you belong to a family that's better dead than alive." Feel free to use it, if you like. I am the old Chinese who made that up.

Hazardous to your health

If you happen to come from Australia, you will probably know what a currawong is. To all others, I offer this: The currawong is a bird, native to Australia, which possesses the unusual ability to mimick the sounds it hears.

At a military base near Sydney some years ago, a flock of currawong (currawongs?) played hob with a company of some 800 men, for the winged creatures learned how to imitate reveille, with the result that the troops were stumbling out of bed at ungodly hours, long before the official call at 6 a.m. This went on for so long that the men became churlish and the company commander was forced to take drastic action. He did, by replacing the reveille bugler with a Scottish bag piper. The birds were rendered silent!

True, the sound of the bag pipes is difficult to imitate. In the opinion of some, this is fortunate. I include, here, a friend who served in World War II with the U.S. 45th Infantry Division. The Division overran a Nazi headquarters unit in the spring of 1945, and among the booty picked up was the regimental drum of the Gordon Highlanders, lost during the retreat of Dunkirk.

Now this drum was highly prized, and finding it was cause for jubilation. It was therefore returned to its rightful owners in colorful ceremonies at Munich shortly after V-E Day. To receive it, the Highlanders sent their superb kilted band. The drummer took back the beloved instrument with a magnificent flourish. Then there were speeches. Long speeches. There was a complete recitation of the regiment's proud and glorious history. Then several American battalions marched by. It was a long day. And hot. And dusty. It ended with the Highlanders band trooping the line, the skirling bag pipes shredding the air with blood-curdling waves of sound.

I prize my friend's letter, written at the time, in which he described the entire incident, ending with: "I hope to Heaven they never lose that damned drum again!"

Let me hasten to state that I am not among those who consider the bag pipe hazardous to human health. One time, years ago, while sailing somewhere on a British ship, I discovered that the pastry chef hailed from Scotland and was an absolute wizard with the pipes. Before that voyage ended I learned so much about the instrument (he even allowed me to try and play it) that I've been a staunch devotee ever since. I remember we got along famously from the start. I said I knew about filling the bag with air and then squeezing it out through the gadget with holes in it but what, for pete's sake, were those three sticks thrusting above his shoulders? "My dear fellow," he answered, "If it weren't for those three sticks the pipes would sound no better than your ordinary piano."

George Bernard Shaw was a great writer. I know, because he told the world so, repeatedly. I've always kept a frigid spot in my heart for him. He was forever taking vicious pokes at America, and one time when he was particularly insulting, a group of newspaper editors returned his fire. One man, from Miami, was especially astute. He knew Shaw was to visit Florida in the near future, and he planned his revenge carefully. At the proper time, a huge story ran in his papers "Mrs. Bernard Shaw did this . . . Mrs. Bernard Shaw said that . . . Mrs. Shaw was entertained yesterday by . . ." Then, down at the bottom, the zinger, the last line: "Mrs. Shaw is being accompanied on her American tour by her husband, a writer."

You are some pumpkin!

Among your other ailments, do you by unhappy chance suffer from an inferiority complex?

If you are one of those who consider themselves so small, so insignificant, so unimportant that they make no waves at all, read on!

If you think of yourself as a mere shadow, clinging to the sidelines, preferring to remain unseen and unheard, this opus is for you.

It is an accepted fact that, from a psychological point of view, there is no such thing as a completely normal person. Everybody suffers from faults and flaws. Striations of weakness weave like ribbons through everyone. The trick, then, is to come as close as possible to normal, to acquire an ego that is the precise size.

Will Rogers put it with eloquent simplicity when he said: "We are all ignorant, only on different subjects." There is another way to say it: Every man is as important as his neighbor, in some respects. There is no need for anyone to feel small, unimportant, insignificant.

A personal illustration—

I do a lot of public speaking, addressing groups as small as 50 people, as large as thousands. I am accustomed to having people come up to me on such occasions and say something like: "I wish I could get up and face a crowd and talk as you do. I wish I had the nerve." Administrators of courses in public speaking, tell me that their first and most difficult task is to destroy the inferiority complex, to give men and women the confidence that supports the realization of their own self-assurance. That's a complicated sentence and I'm not proud of its construction, but I suspect you grasp its meaning.

You will grasp this: I want to tell you a story that will not necessarily thrust you to the top of the heap in whatever you do. It won't shred your inferiority complex, if you have one, nor will it equip you with the assurance required to conquer the world. What it will do, is show you that you are just as important in the scheme of things as the man at your elbow.

A college professor, embarked on a research project, asked a farmer to row him across a stream at a place where there was no bridge. As they progressed, they talked, and a third of the way to the opposite shore the professor asked the farmer if he spoke Greek. When told the rustic did not, the professor said sadly: "You have lost a third of your life." Two thirds of the way across the stream, the professor asked if the farmer spoke Hebrew. Again the answer was negative. "You have lost two thirds of your life." Then the rowboat struck a sharp rock and began to sink, as the farmer asked: "Do you swim?" Alas, the professor could not swim. To which the farmer said, as he jumped into the stream: "Good sir, you have lost all your life."

So thin the thread

Had it not been for a swarm of hungry insects, the United States of America might not be a free and independent nation!

On the face of it, a rather startling statement, wouldn't you say? Yet, entirely true.

As I explain it to you, think back over your own life. Reflect on the events, the decisions, the happenings, that hinged in one way or another on the twists and turns of fate. The time you took the left turn in the road instead of the right, so you met the man who gave you your first job and started you on the road to your career. The time you forgot your hat and so got off the elevator and went back to your office, and so were not on that elevator when it fell to the bottom of the shaft injuring everyone in it. The evening you picked one restaurant over another, went in for dinner and so met the woman who later became your wife.

I can tell you of one man whose life was almost certainly saved by a sneeze. He was in the Army (World War II) and it was during the Battle of the Bulge when all able-bodied troops were being rushed to the front. This soldier one day broke out in a violent spasm of sneezing observed by a nearby officer. He asked what was the trouble and when the enlisted man replied, Hayfever, an action started that led to the soldier's classification as "Limited Service." The man consequently, remained behind while the rest of the unit went into action and was ripped to shreds by the Nazis. Few survived. I can vouch for the authenticity of this episode. I was the soldier who sneezed!

So now, to the swarm of hungry insects. It is safe to say that, had they not played their role in history, the early days of our country might have been drastically altered.

On July 3 in the year 1776, Thomas Jefferson wrote a letter to his wife. "Yesterday, the greatest question was decided which ever was debated in America, and a greater, perhaps, will never be decided among men. The second day of July in 1776 will be the most memorable in the history of America."

As it turned out, Jefferson was a bit too optimistic, a bit premature. For whereas some men were in favor of declaring the independence of the United States from Britain, others greeted the decision differently. Some delegates to the Continental Congress in Philadelphia were apathetic, some lacked the authority to commit themselves, and some simply opposed the move. The argument raged on, through the 3rd of July and into the 4th.

Then, abruptly, all opposition ended, the debate was over, the fateful decision to declare America free was made. Why? What happened to bring about the dramatic reversal? Here are Thomas Jefferson's own words: "The weather was oppressively warm and the room occupied by the deputies was hard by a stable where the flies swarmed thick and fierce, alighting on the legs of the delegates and biting them through their silk stockings. Treason became preferable, to discomfort."

Wisdom is contentment

Have you heard the story of the little boy who went from house to house, selling candy, and when he was asked the purpose of his labors, he said he was raising a million dollars for charity. "That's a lot of money," said a woman. "Do you expect to raise it all by yourself?" "No, ma'am," said the boy. "I got another kid helping me."

Ambition!

Even the young are driven by it. Even they feel its impetus. The more we have, the more we want. The man with a successful business, expands, hires more help, constructs additions, builds branches. The man with one store flourishing, opens a second, a third, finally operates a chain. Success breeds success. More demands more.

But, there are others. I remember when the Guide Michelin awarded three stars to a superb little restaurant in a rural district in France not far from Paris. The owner, far from being delighted with the extraordinary honor bestowed upon his establishment, was distressed. He complained that he would no longer be able to give the dedicated personal attention that he had always lavished upon each customer, because with the spurt of publicity patrons would descend on his restaurant in ever-increasing numbers. One of the assets that had made his business so successful, in the first place, would now be destroyed.

And Al Hartig.

I read about him in the *Wall Street Journal*. Al Hartig and his wife are just about the best kite makers in this country, maybe the world. He quit his job in New York City some years ago and moved to Nantucket, that lovely little island 30 miles off the coast of Massachusetts. There they opened a shop to sell the kites they make.

Mr. Hartig figures that he and his wife make about 5,000 kites each year. He has had requests to produce them in greater quantity; in fact, he has had wholesale orders for as many as 10,000 at one clip, and since his kites sell for as much as $30 each, this would represent an enormous financial gain. But he turned down all these offers. He prefers to sell only what he and Mrs. Hartig can comfortably produce, themselves. They can't begin to meet the demand for their product, but that doesn't bother them. They live comfortably, explaining: "We want to keep the business here where we can run it."

Crazy? Yes, in the eyes of the average business man. But it could be that the Hartigs have learned that a prime aim in life is to get what you want, and next, to enjoy what you have. Only the wisest achieve both. And such wisdom spells genuine contentment.

The Amish

Perhaps, of a Sunday, you took the family for a drive going into the lovely rolling countryside of Lancaster County. If you have, the chances are that at one time or another you found yourself snailing along in a winding line of traffic, held up by one of those funny little horse-drawn buggies driven by the Amish, or the Mennonite Brethren, who live in considerable numbers in that part of Pennsylvania.

Have you ever looked inside one of those little wagons on the road? Have you ever seen the occupants, bearded men in black with wide, flat-brimmed hats, women in dark blue and black with odd-shaped caps on their heads?

I make no pretense at familiarity with the religious beliefs of these sects, but I have enormous respect for these people. You may recall a time when some of the Amish refused to pay certain taxes because they didn't need Social Security assistance then, nor would they accept it ever. Some of their horses were sold by the government to pay those taxes! They are magnificent farmers, these people, but they drive no automobiles, they own no radios, no television, no telephones. They use no electricity, some even shun buttons on their clothing, and of course no zippers. Strange and baffling as these customs are to many, there are firm reasons for them.

Some years ago a severe hurricane (Carol, I think her name was) ravaged this part of Lancaster County and did horrendous damage. I happened to pass through the countryside one week after the storm, and I saw the devastation at first hand.

Carol demolished one barn.

The morning after the hurricane, a group of bearded men appeared at the door of the farmer's home and told him they had come to fix his barn. Some carried hammers, others had saws, picks, shovels; some were brick layers, carpenters, roofers. There were young men, old men, and women who prepared and served food. As the day wore on, more and more arrived until they numbered nearly a hundred. They worked till sundown, and came back day after day until that barn was completely re-built. An absolute minimum of professional assistance was required.

Most important, the farmer who owned the barn was not himself a member of their religious sect. It made no difference. And when the farmer, gazing upon his reconstructed barn in disbelief, asked why they had done this wonderful thing for him, the leader of the group answered very simply: "Why should we not help those in need? It is our religion."

It seems to me there is a profound lesson here for us all.

Prelude to oblivion

America's families are in deep trouble, trouble so deep and pervasive as to threaten the future of our nation . . ."

So began an article in *Time Magazine*, an article that dealt with a situation which, in my opinion, threatens our survival more certainly than all the hydrogen bombs in the world. If all the enemies of the United States were to work in concert plotting our destruction, they could not come up with a horror more effective. And the ghastly part of it is, we are doing this to ourselves. We have no outside help.

The *Time* article concerned the alarming disintegration of the institution we know as The Family. One in four marriages eventually ends in divorce, with the rate rising. In certain sections of California the magazine reported the divorce rate already as high as 70%. Meanwhile, the birth rate has been dropping. The situation is so serious that following a White House Conference on Children, a noted Harvard professor said: "The extinction of faith in the familistic system is identical with the movements in Greece during the century following the Peloponnesian Wars, and in Rome from about the year A.D., 150."

And any student of history will remember that these movements were no less than preludes to the collapse of Greek and Roman civilizations.

The reasons for this staggering state are many and complex and I am not at all capable of offering knowing analyses. But I cannot help uttering a frightened cry of dismay. If the present trend is not reversed, we face a dubious future. Indeed, we may have no future.

A friend said to me one day: "A remarkable thing happened last night. A meeting I was supposed to attend was cancelled, and for the first time in weeks I stayed home. I made an extraordinary discovery. It was marvelous, playing with my children, listening to radio, watching TV. I even read a book, talked to my wife, and fell asleep in my favorite easy chair." He added this: "I learned something I had forgotten, and I'm going to change my way of life. I am applying for membership in the organization known as The Home."

If we do not all apply for membership in The Home, and The Family, there may be nothing else to belong to in the future. The family is the most important single unit of society, and if it disappears we could all go with it into oblivion.

Dr. Paul Popenoe, founder of the American Institute of Family Relations, said at the White House Conference: "No society has ever survived after its family life has deteriorated."

A chilling thought. I wonder, how much time do we have?

The turtle's neck

During lunch with an old friend I hadn't seen in ages, I heard some rather unfamiliar words. He told me about a streak of misfortune that befell him and his family because of something stupid he had done. "Let's face it," he said. "I made a horrible mistake." And it occurred to me, that's an admission hard for the average man to make. *I made a mistake.*

Strange, isn't it, how people will struggle to avoid confessing they made an error? Incredible, the lengths they will go to to cover evidence of mistakes, even to shift the blame to someone else. Three million people go to jail every year in this country for one reason or another. *Somebody* is obviously making mistakes. God knows how many more should be behind bars for the same reason.

Making mistakes is, of course, inevitable. Life is a struggle. The mere process of living suggests we are bound to blunder from time to time. So what's so terrible?

Let me see, how does that old saying go? "A turtle has to stick his neck out to get anywhere."

If a man has vision, if he has ideals, if he dreams, if he has hopes and aspirations, if he is determined to seek for truth, then the risks are even greater, the potential for error is even higher. And the man who does, who moves, who thinks and acts, makes more than mistakes. He makes enemies. As somebody must have chiseled it in stone long ago, the man who makes no enemies makes nothing else either.

Remember Thoreau? He went to jail in protest against what he believed to be unjust taxation. William Penn was imprisoned in the Tower of London for his religious beliefs. Galileo was compelled to bend on his knee before church authorities and deny the validity of a scientific fact. John Wyclif was condemned because he felt that ordinary people should be allowed to read the Bible. Thomas Jefferson was branded as a traitor. Abraham Lincoln was ridiculed by his enemies and called a baboon. Woodrow Wilson was labeled a traitor in the White House.

To this galaxy, we could add many more names. We could speak of those of our own day who have been condemned, persecuted—yes, murdered!—because of their beliefs and convictions.

We are not all given to walk upon the world's stage in the company of such greats as Jefferson and Lincoln and Martin Luther King, but each of us in his own way runs the daily risk of making mistakes. And enemies. They are by-products of living, and there seems to be no way to escape the problem.

There is nothing wrong with making mistakes. The only wrong is the refusal to acknowledge a mistake when we make it.

As a man thinks

Scientists tell us that the Planet Earth is about three billion years old. Crushing as the weight of that figure is, it represents a mere pinpoint in the contemplation of a Universe so colossal that it takes two billion years for the light to reach us from distant galaxies, even though that light is flowing toward our telescopes at the rate of six trillion miles a year!

All this, everything that is happening in the Universe, scientists explain, is regulated by eternal laws that are so exact, so precise, that predictions can be made centuries ahead. And much can be told of what happened eons in the past. The precise moment for each sunrise, sunset, eclipse—the ebb and flow of tides. All these are governed by laws as inexorable as time itself.

What is certainly as amazing, is that people—we—are also governed by laws, and I am here of course not referring to the man-made variety. I am thinking of the laws that in their most simplistic form are recorded in the Bible. Namely: "As a man thinketh in his heart, so is he."

At some moment in the dim reaches of past ages, the greatest invention of all came into being, the alphabet. When it was discovered that it was possible to devise symbols representing the sounds made by the human voice, language resulted. Man learned to communicate.

And then a tremendous problem confronted him. For he then possessed the power to make a choice.

If you consider language, words, the alphabet, as a tool, a piece of equipment, then you can realize that man must make the decision whether to use that tool for his benefit, or for his destruction.

Nothing man-made exists that did not spring first from the human mind!

Look around you. Everything you see that was made by man *is* because at some point it was conceived in the mind of man. It is one of the inexorable laws of our Universe. So it is clear that nothing can affect us so profoundly as what goes on inside the heads and hearts of men and women everywhere. It has always been so. It will always be so.

The Earth is three billion years old. Somewhere, somehow, man invented his alphabet and started putting sentences together as the capacity for thought developed. And then man realized that the Divine power that had brought him thus far, had also given to him the need, and the power, to make a choice.

As we think, we are.

The jig is up

Several old-timers were sitting around the pot-bellied stove recalling the old days out west, and the Indians. One old codger said he'd never forget the time he got his first Indian, and when a companion asked if he shot him, he said: "Nope."

"I suppose," supposed another, "you got him in hand-to hand fighting?"

"Nothing like that," replied the old-timer. "I ran him to death."

"Really? How far did you chase him?"

"Didn't," came the answer. "I was in front."

Will anybody mind if I write about the American Indian in a light vein, for a change? He is, beyond question, one of the most tragic figures on our history pages, but there are some charming stories in my files and if they provoke a chuckle, it won't do any harm, will it?

There was, for instance, the Indian chief, head of a tribe in Nevada, who was worth a stack of money. Also, he was a compulsive gambler. So one day he hopped into his car and drove to Las Vegas for a swing at the casinos. As luck would have it, he didn't have any. Luck, that is. He was wiped clean. In the morning he climbed to the top of the nearest tall mountain and sent a series of smoke signals back to his tribe asking for more money. The tribe warily signalled back: "Why you want extra money?" But before the chief could reply, the Atomic Energy Commission set off an atomic bomb in the desert and a huge mushroom cloud billowed upward to the top of the sky. Immediately the tribe smoked the message: "Okay! Okay, we're sending the money. Only stop screaming!"

Years ago, I found the copy of an essay written by a school-boy as a class assignment. His teacher had asked him to write about the discovery of America by Columbus, and this masterpiece resulted:

"Columbus was a smart guy who could make an egg stand on one end without breaking, so one day the King of Spain who was married to a woman named Isabel sent for him and said can you discover America, and Columbus said sure, if you get me some boats. So he got some boats and sailed in the direction where he knew America was, and the sailors mutinied and said there was no such a place but finally the pilot yelled Columbus, land is in sight. When the boat got near shore Columbus saw some natives and he asked them is this America and they said yes so he said I guess we made it and one native said we're Indians and you are Columbus, I take it. And when Columbus said yes I am one Indian turned to the other and said well chief I guess the jig is up, we are discovered at last."

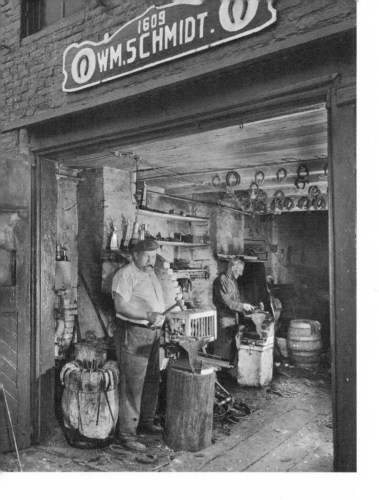

Who gets the credit?

As I understand it, you were involved in some kind of important project, right? You worked hard on it, put in a lot of long, tough hours. You worked overtime, skipped meals, and lost sleep worrying about whether or not you could have done better. You poured yourself into the task and pushed till it was finished, and then you sat back and watched—as someone else got all the credit.

That *has* happened to you, hasn't it?

Of course. It's happened to everyone. Not the most pleasant of experiences, but then who said life wasn't vexing at times? The best way to handle a situation like that is to have a quick snort (if you drink) and then forget the whole thing. Keep it inside and it'll bug the daylights out of you.

Somebody once said that who wins the battle isn't half as important as that the battle was won. Okay. Nice words. But if they still don't convince you, get this:

It was a summer day in the year 1777. Three men came galloping up to a blacksmith shop in a small Vermont village. One of the horses was limping badly, but all the able-bodied men in town had gone to join General Stark and his embattled forces at Bennington, so there was nobody to help that horse but a fifteen year old crippled boy by the name of Luke Varnum.

The three men were distressed. No blacksmith, and time was of the essence! "I can help," said the crippled lad, explaining that he had been helping his father, that he could shoe that horse. "I know what to do, really I do. I'll get the fire going in the forge and you bring the horse inside."

The men hesitated, but there was no alternative. They were at the mercy of the young cripple.

Luke worked quickly, quietly, efficiently. He removed the shoe, fit the horse with a new rim of metal, driving it fast with strong nails pounded in just right. Luke had even made those nails himself. When the job was done, the men paid the boy for his services, then mounted their horses and galloped away.

The man whose horse needed the special care was Seth Warner. Colonel Seth Warner. And if you will check, you will find that history gives Colonel Warner the credit for racing to Bennington, bringing reinforcements just in the nick of time to join General Stark and his men, just in time to turn the tide of battle and bring a victory to the hard-pressed Revolutionary army. That is the way history tells it.

But there were others.

There were those who said that Colonel Seth Warner was not that day's hero. They said the credit for turning the tide of battle really should have gone to a fifteen year old crippled boy by the name of Luke Varnum.

Dignity

He was walking toward me on the city street, and I saw him from afar. Even at a distance, I was impressed with his gait, the tilt of his head, his overall manner. What dignity! Closer, to my surprise, I recognized him. Homburg hat, glistening black shoes, a superbly tailored greatcoat with fur at the collar. It was the world renowned architect, Eward Durrell Stone.

Genuine dignity, of course, has nothing to do with externals. With clothing. It is an inner thing with no relation whatsoever to material possessions. It stems from the deepest fibres of the being.

"Nobility, or elevation of character . . ." is what the dictionary says. This is the real dignity.

This is the great Albert Schweitzer, sitting down to a collapsing piano in the steaming jungles of Africa, filling the festering heat of his battered hospital with music of incandescent beauty. This is Marie, the incredibly poor woman who came daily to my back door to sell chickens for twenty cents each the year I spent several months on the island of Haiti; Marie, who wore the same filthy rags day after day, never owned a pair of shoes in her life, and to whom a dollar was a fortune; Marie, whose noble character shone like a beacon in the smile on her tired black face.

And this was Rabbi Rabinowitz.

Rabbi Rabinowitz lived over a grocery store on the Lower East Side of New York City years ago. He had been a poor man all his life, but a man of great, imperturbable dignity. He served his small, poor congregation with unflagging dedication, and so that those who needed him might find him, there was a sign in the window of the store that read: "Rabbi Rabinowitz Is Upstairs."

When he died, his friends wanted to erect a stone memorial on his grave. They did, selecting one that reflected the noble character of the man, one that bespoke the same quiet dignity which had always been his hallmark. It was a simple stone, severely plain, and on it were cut these words: "Rabbi Rabinowitz Is Upstairs."

Stop, Look and Learn!

What do you know today that you didn't know yesterday?

Think on that for a moment. Roll that question around in
your mind. What did you learn in the last twenty-four hours? In what
way have you added to your store of knowledge? Have you widened any
of your horizons, increased the depth of your vision and understanding,

thrown fresh light on cloudy areas of ignorance, or do you stand precisely in the same spot you stood yesterday?

Learning, we sometimes automatically assume, is the business of the young. Wrong! The young go to school, sure, where they are supposed to be educated. But the man or woman of any age who seeks the riches of life must continue the process of learning or he fails miserably.

Happily, many realize this.

We frequently read of grandmothers who troop off to college to earn a degree, middle aged men and women who study at night school, people of all strata who thirst for knowledge. I find this heart warming. I applaud these persons. They understand the value of education and climb over whatever obstacles there are to get it.

But of course it is not necessary to go to school to learn. Formal education is only one source of knowledge.

I know a man who taught himself the Italian language, however flimsily, when he was in his 70's. I know a woman who was in her mid-40's when she decided she wanted to know how to play the piano and began taking lessons. I know a man, a college professor with absolutely no knowledge to equip himself for the task, who learned how to build (and built!) a beautiful home in which he and his family are now living, and except for a few assists from electrical and plumbing experts he did the whole job himself. I know a man, already well established in one field, who is becoming a skilled vintner, while his wife has veered off at an oblique angle to become an equally qualified gardener. I know a man who determined at the age of 55 to teach himself the art of the silversmith, and now at 57 has a reputation that threatens to grow to national dimensions. I know a woman who taught herself all about growing camellias, and now, in her late 60's, she is one of this country's leading florists specializing in this exotic flower.

I could go on, but you get the point.

What do *you* know this week that you didn't know last week? Are you now exactly where you were then, or have you added some new vision to your life?

Don't tell me there's no point in learning, especially if one is "up in years." Because I'll hurl back at you a fistful of words by a very wise man. Aristotle. When asked the advantage of knowledge, he said: "It is an ornament to a man in prosperity and a refuge to him in adversity."

The gift to yourself

On the outskirts of a town in the state of Maine, you will find a road sign. Six markers, pointing arrows, are fixed to it, listing other communities and the miles of road winding to them. From the top, they are: Freedom—45 miles. Liberty—33 miles. Harmony—96 miles. Unity—52 miles. Union—20 miles. Hope—27 miles.

Freedom.
Liberty.
Harmony.
Unity.
Union.
Hope.

And the name of the town at the fringe of which you will find this road sign? Friendship!

It is, of course, sheer geographical coincidence that those six marvelously named towns should be within easy driving distance of Friendship. But it is not coincidence that friendship, with a small F, can lead to freedom and liberty for individuals, produce harmony, unity and union, and generate hope. Friendship inspires miracles, just as its opposite promotes fear, distrust, suspicion, destruction.

I recall an incredible incident that took place in India a few years ago. A bus carrying eighty-six passengers was trapped by flood waters along a rampaging river 100 miles southwest of Delhi. Karim Khan, a merchant from a nearby community, swam out to the bus carrying a rope which he had anchored to a truck on high ground. He told the passengers to pull themselves to safety along the rope, and eight, did.

But in India, the caste system has been so deeply ingrained in the pattern of life, that the remaining seventy-eight passengers who were members of a higher-caste community, refused to share the same rope. They elected to remain on the bus. The waters rose higher, and in moments, the bus was swept away. Seventy-eight men and women lost their lives.

Illogical?

But all prejudice is illogical. By definition. And though it may not destroy as violently, as dramatically, it inevitably leads through misunderstanding and distrust to destruction.

Lafcadio Hearn tells of an incident in the Orient. Through the selfless bravery of one man, the lives of many neighbors were saved. For this, the neighbors visited their Shinto temples regularly to worship his spirit, even though he was still alive.

What magnificent logic!

"A friend," said Robert Louis Stevenson, "is a gift you give to yourself."

We can find our way to freedom, liberty, harmony, unity, union and hope—through friendship. It is a gift we must all give to ourselves. There is no other road.

The common need

A little girl—a fifth grader—once described loneliness as "having no one with whom to share your happiness." It would be difficult to improve on that definition, wouldn't you say?

During a vacation trip to New England, I visited an old friend. He was at his summer place along the coast, and I found him puttering in his garden. He is a well known art critic who lives in New York City most of the year, and to my dismay I learned that, since I had last seen him, his wife had died and he was quite alone.

I sensed a great sadness in him as we talked, all the more pronounced since I knew him as a man of enormous enthusiasm and zest for life, with a lively capacity for humor. I tried to speak words of comfort, but I was not too surprised when he suddenly said that the truth of the matter was that nobody could help him, fate had kicked him in the teeth and left him horribly lonely. "I am surrounded by friends," he said, "but you know it is possible to live in the largest city in the country and have swarms of friends and still suffer with the most awful loneliness."

I knew he was right.

And just as certainly, I feel that those who are more fortunate, those whose days are bright and happy and filled with hope and joy, have the responsiblity for sharing those treasures with others. They all have one common need. No, I must amend that: *we* all have that common need.

I can never forget Linda.

She was eight years old, and she lived in an orphanage. She was small and shy and unattractive, and she was regarded as something of a problem child. That she was alive at all was really a miracle, for she had suffered horribly in her first years at the hands of cruel, inhuman parents.

Linda saw other children of her age leaving the orphanage, going out into foster homes, being adopted, being given new lives. She saw her little friends going out into the big, strange world to join new brothers and sisters, mothers and fathers, in a quest for joy and happiness.

But nobody wanted Linda. She remained at the orphanage.

Now there was a rule at the institution that any letters written by the children had to be approved before they were posted. Linda knew this rule, and yet one day she was seen stealing down to the main gate and carefully hiding what looked like a letter in a tree. One of the attendants, a young woman, hurried to that tree to retrieve the envelope and open it.

Her eyes filled with tears as she read little Linda's note: "To anyone who finds this—I Love You."

The power of hate

One day while working on a radio script dealing with the power of hate, I turned to a reference book in my library to see what I could find relative to that four-letter word. It was really no surprise to discover that in example after example I was directed by the indexes to the same sources I found when I was seeking quotes on the subject of "war."

This is no accident.

There is a definite link between the hatred that individual men and women carry in their hearts and that incredible phenomenon called war that has been plaguing mankind for eons. After all, nations are made up of people, individuals, and if they are conditioned to hatred and the power of hate, there is no reason to expect them to behave differently, collectively, as a nation.

Oddly, there are many who don't grasp this at all. They rail against war and label it "immoral" yet see nothing wrong in nursing hatred in their hearts for real and imagined wrongs done them by others.

We could indulge in sermonizing about the power of hate as opposed to the healing power of love, we could cry from the rooftops that until *all* men banish hate from their lives we can never know peace among the peoples of the world. But nothing could match in effectiveness and directness the story of something that happened during World War 2 when an American warship in the Pacific took some wounded Japanese prisoners aboard. One of the American medical officers took care of these prisoners, took such excellent care of them, in fact, that his fellow officers became quite indignant.

One day this annoyance on the part of his colleagues reached the explosive point, and one of the men exclaimed: "Let 'em die, for pete's sake! Throw 'em below decks and let 'em die the way they let our men die!" The doctor waited patiently until the tirade had ended. "Are you finished?" he asked quietly. "Tell me, did you go to mass on Sunday?"

"Yes. But what does that have to do with—?"

"Did you go to confession beforehand?"

"Yes."

"You say you're a member of a Christian church?"

"Yes, but—"

"You're a damned hypocrite!" The ward room grew tense. "Let me tell you something. I play the game according to the rules of decency, even if others don't. And I'm going to continue that way. The Japanese war lords told their men that all Americans are beasts. One of these days these wounded prisoners will return home and they will know their leaders lied to them. They will be able to say they were treated with kindness and compassion by an officer who cared for them as human beings. I'm going to replace the hatred in their hearts with something else. Love, if possible. Because I'm convinced that's the only way we're ever going to have peace in this world. Now, do you have anything to say?"

Walking the plank

Here's an interesting experiment you may want to try: Get a strong plank of wood, at least four inches wide and six feet long. Place it on the floor of a room, and then walk on it from end to end.

Easy?

Now, elevate that plank at least a foot off the floor, by supporting each end on some object such as a chair. It's still easy to walk from one end of that plank to the other without falling off, isn't it? Sure. But now elevate the plank still more, say six feet, by placing each end on a step ladder. Think you can still do it?

If you hesitate, think of construction workers, the men who put up skyscrapers and walk nonchalantly on girders with nothing but space between them and the ground below. How do they do it?

What happens when you raise your plank? Why can you walk it on the ground, not when it's suspended in the air? It's the same plank. You're using the same muscles, the same mind, the same will. You're covering the same distance.

The difference is that when the plank is on the ground, you think only of walking. When it's elevated, you think of falling. Your sense of balance goes askew.

A mind burdened with fear, is troubled, has also gone askew. A heart heavy with doubt, carrying the notion of failing rather than succeeding, has a severe problem. The man whose sense of balance wobbles between achievement and disaster, courts doom.

Remember these words by Thomas a Kempis:

"Be not angry that you cannot make others as you wish them to be, for you cannot make yourself as you wish to be."

To become what one is capable of being can be an awesome task. It can require fierce dedication. It may call for great effort. It could demand intense concentration.

A Michigan newspaper published a list of our greatest possessions. Perusal of this list, it seems to me, might help us to achieve a workable balance and a clearer view of our aims:

"The best day is Today. The greatest sin is Fear. The best gift is Forgiveness. The greatest mistake is Giving Up. The greatest need is Common Sense. The most expensive indulgence is Hate. The greatest troublemaker is Talking Too Much. The greatest deceiver is He Who Deceives Himself. The greatest loss is No Enthusiasm. The stupidest thing to do is Find Fault. The best teacher is Learning. The warmest feeling is Gratitude. The greatest possession is Abiding Faith."

Concentrate on these. I don't guarantee you'll be able to walk a plank suspended high above the ground, but you'll have a fine sense of balance. And that's mighty important.

The dimensions of greatness

During one of his countless American concert tours, Ignace Paderewski, the eminent Polish pianist, was persuaded to audition a young lady who felt she had enormous musical talent. He sat through her bumbling performance, trying to hide his boredom, and when she had finished the young player asked: "What do I do now?" Paderewski sighed and said: "Get married."

Paderewski was a remarkable man. He conquered the world as a concert pianist. He was so successful that he became one of the few artists ever to travel about this country in his own private railroad car. Yet, when he was at the peak of his career as a musician, he turned to international politics, to become the head of government of his native Poland.

There were times when he mixed careers, functioning in both capacities simultaneously. He died in 1941, shortly after returning to the United States, a land he loved deeply, and whose people loved him warmly in return.

There have been many wonderful stories told about him, but the one I like best and which gives great insight into his character, goes back to a time when he played a private concert for Queen Victoria in England. At the end of the evening the Queen took his hand and exclaimed with enthusiasm: "Paderewski, you are a genius."

"Perhaps, Majesty . . ." replied the pianist. "But before I became a genius, I was a drudge."

He knew that before you could experience fame, you had to work for it. He knew that fame didn't come without effort. He knew that before you could scale the heights as a pianist (or a politician) you had to wade through the marshland below.

Paderewski knew what those before him, and since, have learned the hard way: nothing of value comes without paying the purchase price. And he knew one thing more, a requisite for a career as an artist, a politician, or just about any other endeavor you can name. You have to care for people! Perhaps it would be more accurate to say, you have to *love* people.

On one of his many American concert tours, Paderewski appeared in a midwestern town. The house was packed, as always, and when the final encore was played the applause was still deafening. Yet Paderewski was disturbed. An assistant asked him, backstage, what was troubling him. "Some friends were missing tonight," he answered. "Two gray-haired people who always sit in the same seats in the second row every time I play in this town."

"I didn't know you had any friends here," said his aide.

"I don't," Paderewski replied. "I have never met them, but I have seen them in the audience, I have played for them for twenty years, and they weren't in the audience tonight. I hope there is nothing seriously wrong."

Can anyone wonder why he is still, even today, always referred to as the *great* Paderewski?

We travel the world

S

pend your vacation in your own backyard," said the squib in *The Reader's Digest.* "Your friends will know that you are sensible, imaginative, resourceful, home-loving—and broke."

Maybe so.

But there is another way to consider this. Let me explain by telling you of a church I sometimes pass when I am out walking. Not a very striking edifice, architecturally speaking, I had seen it countless times. I had passed it without thinking, usually in the late afternoon or early evening. Then one day I walked by this church in the morning, on a day when the sun was shining brightly, shining on the opposite side of the building, *through* the interior, emerging in a set of magnificent stained glass windows. I stood in disbelief on the sidewalk! How often had I walked there, yet until that moment I had never been aware of those windows! In a new light, a new perspective, all that beauty was revealed to me. It was there, all the time, but I had not seen it.

So often this is the case. Wonders beyond imagination are all around us, but because they are always there, we take them for granted.

A dear friend of mine is a lecturer. He makes his own motion pictures and uses them to illustrate talks he gives all over the country. His films are fabulous, audiences go wild over them, they have earned countless awards, they have built a national reputation for him. And yet—get this!—more than 80% of all the film he has exposed has been to capture miracles of nature within a radius of a few hundred feet of the house in which he lives!

His subjects? Flowers, trees, birds, *grass.* You see, he uses "delayed action" photography, revealing in a few moments the complete life cycle of, say, one single daisy. His screen, in vivid color, depicts the four seasons parade of a solitary tree. With telescopic lens, he opens human eyes to the habits of the common sparrow.

He has a fresh view, a new perspective.

So maybe you spend your vacation at home because you are broke. Perhaps the circumstances of your life restrict your wanderings. No matter. There is no reason to be without the rich beauties that cover this earth. They are here, they are ours for the taking.

I suspect you remember Emerson's words on this subject. It is well to recall them clearly: "Though we travel the world over to find the beautiful, we must carry it with us, or we find it not."

The nearest hero

Consider, please, these four names: Thomas Welch, Elliott Handler, Margaret Rudkin, John Hand.
You say you've never heard of them?

Maybe so, but wait. Dr. Thomas Welch enjoyed having a glass of wine, but for medical reasons was unable to drink it. So he began experimenting with grapes in his kitchen at home. The result—Welch's Grape Juice.

Elliott Handler began fiddling around with tools at his workbench, making doll furniture in his spare time. The products of his labor were so professional that before he knew what was happening he was President of Mattel, the largest maker of toys in the world.

Margaret Rudkin had a neighbor who enjoyed homemade bread, so she went into her kitchen to whip up a batch, using an old family recipe and a stove she found in her attic. The bread she made was so delicious that a new industry was born—Pepperidge Farm.

Three plain, ordinary people who knew how to do something exceptionally well. And so they grew to be famous, and almost certainly rich. They had something to give. They gave. Society was happy to have them.

But I gave you four names, remember? The fourth was John Hand. His story, too, is fascinating.

In the Los Altos hills, south of San Francisco, the name of John Hand is known to a great many people. And they are very grateful to him. A former Marine, with a friendly, cheerful manner, he is now (or was, anyway, when this was written) a postman. He covers a 50-mile route and the countryside through which he passes is a constant blaze of beauty because, in all the years he has worked for the Government, he has been gathering flower seeds, tucking them into little capsules along with a touch of fertilizer, and scattering them from his mail truck as he makes his rounds. Where once there was only bare earth, or clumps of weeds growing in arrid, dusty country, there are now bright, beautiful, colorful flower plants. His efforts to beautify the land don't interfere with his work, and everyone, including his superiors at the Post Office, is mighty proud of him. Both his father and grandfather were horticulturists, but he feels that beauty should not be confined to the greenhouse.

I suspect you never heard of John Hand. I suspect, further, that he has not grown one penny richer for his efforts. And probably couldn't care less. The point is, he too has something to give, and he is giving. He is helping to brighten the corner of the world where he lives. He is doing something, however small, to improve the lot of society. John Hand will not amass fame and fortune making grape juice, or toys, or bread, but his contribution is as important nonetheless.

To find your nearest hero, look around you. He may be at your elbow.

The seed of forever

There once was a woman who acknowledged no Divine power, no force or purpose other than her own accidental existence. She was an atheist.

No one knew this woman's full background. No one knew what pressures and influences had combined, in her earlier years, to shape her into what she was. And no one really cared. She had lived her life according to the dictates of her own will, the only law she recognized. In her world, she alone was god.

It was natural, then, that this woman would be disliked by many. Despised, really. And it was natural that when she fell ill there would be little genuine concern expressed for her welfare. She had laughed at her neighbors, scoffed them, scorned them. She had proclaimed herself the supreme being, an egotist unmatched in the community. She had denied the concept of God and the hereafter. She had attempted to make a mockery of those who believed otherwise.

No one knew with what spirit she approached her own last reckoning, for when her illness deepened, she died alone. She who somehow had felt herself above all others, suffered the fate of mere mortals. In due time she was buried.

Now this woman had left specific instructions that her grave was to be covered with a slab of solid granite, in turn surrounded by heavy blocks of stone. In her defiance, she was savagely determined that man would remember her. She wanted everyone to know the exact location of her final resting place. In years to come they would always be able to find the spot, and think of her.

But it happened that not far from her grave, there stood an oak tree. And one day a squirrel, while gathering acorns against the coming winter, dropped one of the nuts. It fell to the ground at the very edge of the huge stone that covered this woman's grave. In time, it took root and sprouted. There had been cold and rain and howling wind and deep snow, but then spring came and the sun lavished its life-giving rays upon the earth, and as a plant grows in a wall of concrete where its grasping roots find a bit of earth, so a tiny sapling appeared. The cycle of life was beginning again.

In that strange, mysterious and awesome way that life develops, this acorn began its upward climb, slowly, powerfully, in a surge that eventually moved the huge stones from their base. And as the years passed and the tree's roots dug even deeper and as its trunk thrust ever higher, the massive granite itself was split in two.

In time, the marking on this woman's grave, the remainder of her existence, was gone. And in its place stook a towering oak, rising in majestic splendor, its branches reaching, as in prayer, to the skies.

Digging a ditch?

Three men began their working lives as ditch diggers. They were of about the same age, came from the same section of the city, and all performed the same hard labor.

One day, an elderly man came by the place these three men were working, and for a time he stood there watching. Finally, he turned to the nearest of the three and asked him what he was making.

The man, without looking up, replied: "Eight dollars a day."

The passerby smiled, turned to the second fellow and asked him the same question: "Excuse me, sir, but what are you making?" His answer was a surly: "What does it look like I'm making? I'm digging a ditch."

The old gentleman then turned to the third worker, whose name was Bill, and asked what he was making. The fellow put down his shovel, looked up and replied: "What am I making? I'm making a cathedral."

Time passed.

Years later, in the same city, those three men were still working. Only two, however, were still digging ditches. The third, Bill, sat in his office high in a downtown skyscraper, a prosperous business man. From his desk he could look down into the street where his erstwhile colleagues still labored with pick and shovel. From his comfortable office he could almost hear them as they grumbled: "Bill sure was lucky. He got all the breaks."

Whatever we do, however lowly the task, our eyes should be focused above and beyond to a greater goal. There is nothing wrong with digging ditches. No task is insignificant, only the man who performs it. He can lend dignity to his work, or rob it of meaning.

If a man merely goes through the motions of working, putting in a set number of hours each day, no more no less, asking in return a set number of dollars—if this is all he sees in his labors, then his vision is blurred and his aims are dulled. If he looks beyond the immediate task, beyond the hours, the pay, the material reward, if he sees a goal that is larger than himself and the work he is accomplishing, then he is on the track for the greatest kind of satisfaction.

Harry Emerson Fosdick once said that a genuinely good life involves going all out for worthwhile causes and trying to leave the world a little better because we were born into it.

I like to think that a man like Bill in our little modern allegory knew how to live a genuinely good life.

It's a good question, one we might all ask ourselves each morning as we begin the day's toil: "What am *I* doing? Digging a ditch, or building a cathedral?"

Having and making

Remember Margaret Lee Runbeck and her charming "Miss Boo" stories? In one of them, she told of two little boys, one nine years old, the other seven, who decided to build a little cart to haul each other around in. When the rickety contraption was almost completed the one, Mike, said: "Which do you think is more fun, making or having?" The other child, Bill, sat in the sawdust for a while, pondering, then he decided: "Making."

There's a whole mountain of wisdom in that story.

Why does a man buy seeds, break his back digging in his garden, spend weeks in futile combat with weeds, carry water in dry weather to his plants, spray against insects and disease, all to produce by midsummer a handful of tomatoes that he could buy for a fraction of the cost, even with inflation, at the nearest store? Or receive as a gift from his neighbors?

Why does a man with no facility whatsoever with hammer and saw, struggle in his workshop risking battered thumbs and splinters and assorted contusions, all to assemble a bookcase that no self-respecting wife would consign to any spot but the attic, when he could purchase a handsome and functional piece of furniture that would last for years as the pride of the living room?

Because making is more fun than having.

When you have, a need is filled. Filled, yet there is a void, an emptiness. Motivation is suspended. Having, is an external circumstance, while making comes from within. It is the result of the creative drive. As long as these wheels are in motion, there is purpose. When this stops, something inside dies.

I once spent a delightful hour or so watching two small boys, a bit younger than those Miss Runbeck had in mind, at play. Their home was filled with toys of every description, some expensive and sturdy, but how did they spend their time? In the utility room, happily driving nails in to a block of wood. They were making something. They didn't know what, and couldn't care less, and when they had filled that wood with as many nails as it would hold, they chucked it aside and started on a new block. Making was more fun than having.

I could drop the subject here, find a nice bunch of words to wrap things up, but I won't. I'm going to take the matter a bit further and suggest that maybe this is the reason so many retirements go sour. Maybe this is why so many men reach the gold watch stage, settle into days of nothingness, then drop dead. While they are working they are creating, they are making, and when they retire they are having, living on the accumulated resources of the past. I can lean on the beliefs of no great authority to support my theory; I have no statistical evidence to back my notion. I am certain only that with attainment, need evaporates. And when this happens, man's mind becomes fallow. That's when trouble starts.

Sincerely yours

Pheidias was very likely the greatest sculptor the land of ancient Greece produced. Legend tells that when he was working on the statute of Diana which was to adorn the Acropolis in Athens, a passerby noticed that he was laboring with extreme care, applying his chisel to the rear side of Diana's head, shaping each strand of hair with great patience, with attention to the most minute detail.

The observer reminded Pheidias that the statue would stand a hundred feet high with its back to the marble wall. "Who," he asked, "will ever appreciate the fruits of your efforts? Who will ever know such beauty is there?"

And Pheidias replied: "*I* will know."

That story, as I see it, illustrates a human characteristic of inestimable value. It might be called self-respect. Possibly integrity. For the moment, I choose to label it—Sincerity. Unflagging, all-pervading, unceasing sincerity, always doing what is right, always acknowledging truth. It has been said that we will never be any more than we are when nobody is looking, and if you possess the degree of sincerity Pheidias had, you will do what you have to do regardless of those who may be watching, regardless of the fact that nobody may be watching.

I like to think we are all born sincere. Show me the young child who isn't! The trick is to keep it. It is only as we grow older that we learn to employ deceit, that we find "virtue" in bending the truth.

The man who is consistently sincere avoids carloads of trouble. He misses packs of headaches and worry, he can keep his cool in most any situation, he doesn't need a good memory in order to recall what lies he may have told. What he *is* is apparent in what he says.

Yes, sincerity can be faked. For a while. Like a wig, slipped on to simulate age, someone with a modicum of theatrical experience can give the impression of being sincere. But in time the outer shell wears off, like layers of paint peeling from a barn too long exposed to the elements.

Sincerity is a quality to be admired in everyone. Whether you have it or not is determined by your willingness to live by your principles. Whether you work with your hands, or your mind, or both, do you adhere unfailingly to the truth as you see it? Do you produce the best of which you are capable whether anyone is looking or not?

Material possessions, even wealth, are comparatively easy to give away, but when a man gives the gift of his daily life through principle, you have conclusive evidence that he is indeed sincere.

The crystal ball

M y fee", said the fortune teller, "is twenty-five dollars. For that amount you may ask two questions."

"My!" exclaimed the client. "Isn't that a lot of money for just two questions?"

"Yes," replied the fortune teller. "Now what's your second question?"

Man's concern for the future, actually, is no laughing matter. Despite the total absence of all firm evidence that channels into tomorrow exist, we continue to spend a lot of time and effort and energy —and money—in the vain quest for a glimpse of what is to come. Today, this desire for knowledge of the future is more acute than ever. Occultism is big business. Dissatisfaction with the here and now is driving people in ever increasing numbers to a hoped-for peep at the perhaps and maybe.

Lucus Annaeus Seneca, the Roman philosopher, dramatist and statesman, who was born in the year 3 B. C., said that the mind that's anxious about the future, is miserable today.

He was right.

I rather imagine he and Blaise Pascal would have had a serious tangle of tongues, for the Frenchman, who was precocious as a child and a subscriber to mysticism later in life, felt that man should occupy himself with concern for the future; the past and present are means to an end, and the future is the only end. Thus we never live, we only hope to live.

Me, I have faith in the future. I figure it's going to be here in ten minutes, I'm going to do my level best to prepare for it, but beyond that I can't get too shook up. I don't want to know about tomorrow. I'll meet it when it arrives. I'll cope.

This whole train of thought started rattling through my mind when I was walking downtown one evening and I came to one of those seedy joints you find in all big cities, the dingy emporiums run by fortune tellers, tea leaf analysts, palm readers and other so-called "advisors" who claim to have an eye or an ear tuned to next day. As I paused to survey the establishment, the proprietor (the prophetess herself, I suspect) appeared from behind a beaded curtain and beckoned coyly, "Come in!"

Now I realize that a lot of people patronize these purveyors of posterity, and I have no wish to deprive them of one moment of satisfaction, but as that woman crooked her finger and urged me in for a glimpse at my future, I couldn't help but remember a story I once heard:

A man paid a visit to a fortune teller and found the bearded prophet sitting at a table on which rested a crystal ball. The man noticed that the ball had two holes in it, and he asked: "How come?"

"Every Tuesday night," said the fortune teller, "I go bowling."

J. C. Penney was in his nineties when he said: "My eyesight is impaired, but my vision is better than ever." Get the message? Age has no bearing on this vision. I'm sure you know people, as I do, who plod around the little circles of their existence, never raising their eyes above the horizon. They're unhappy, hemmed in by walls of their own futility. Others are never bogged down by hardship, they never falter, with chin up they climb, eyes on the stars. They know the sun will always gild the mountaintop before it shines on the plain They understand that we see facts with our eyes, ideas with our minds, and ideals with our souls.

The tall tree

Possibly you have heard the story of the woman who made artificial fruit of such perfection that it was almost impossible by just looking to detect the difference between it and the real thing.

Her skill was so remarkable that she was urged to make the fruit for sale, and eventually people came from far and wide to purchase her creations. It was then the critics appeared. Some found fault with the coloring of her fruit, others the shape, still others the size. One day when there were a number of customers in her shop, one man became harshly critical of a big bowl of red, juicy looking apples. Weary of his tirade, the woman who made the fruit calmly picked up one of the apples, sliced it with a knife and ate it.

It was a real apple.

No matter how perfect, there will always be someone to criticize. It's comforting to escape the critic's cutting edge, but almost impossible. There will always be someone who knows better, or thinks he does, and find fault with what you do. An old proverb puts it succinctly: The tall tree catches the most wind.

The only practical thing to do is to expect criticism from the start. Brace yourself against it. And realize that some of the criticism may be justified, the rest worthless. Pray for the wisdom to know the difference.

There is an old story that has taken many forms. The way I heard it first, it concerned a poet who lived in ancient Persia.

The poet went walking through the countryside one day accompanied by his son and his donkey. A neighbor who happened along noticed that the old man and the boy were perspiring profusely in the hot sun, while the donkey contentedly nibbled grass, so he said: "How foolish you are to walk, when you could ride." So the poet and the youngster climbed onto the donkey and rode through the next village, where a woman saw them and said: "You ought to be ashamed, forcing that poor animal to carry the two of you." So the poet dismounted and walked, while the son rode. Whereupon a passing tradesman said: "Poor old man, walking, while the youth rides in comfort." They changed places. The poet rode, the son walked. And this provoked a merchant in the marketplace to say: "Just look at the father, at ease, while the boy is forced to walk. For shame!"

Ah, yes, you too have walked with your son and your donkey, haven't you?

It might help to remember the observation of Fred Allen. "If criticism really hurt, the skunk would have disappeared long ago."

The rat race starts Wednesday

A magazine I read regularly publishes classified advertising, and I never miss this section. I find it fascinating, especially those items labeled *Personal*. In one of these columns I discovered an advertisement for an organization that teaches, by mail, how to meditate. It suggests that meditation invokes knowledge and insight, and it urges all who would gain these treasures to write for full details. The fount of this wisdom is located in (where else?) California.

Now I must confess I never thought I might have to *learn how* to meditate. The lofty plateau of transcendental meditation was meant for others, who could have it, and I would require the services of a guru about as frequently as I would need a personal phrenologist. I thought meditation came about as easily as breathing.

But I do agree that meditation invokes knowledge and insight. In fact, it invokes a whale of a lot more.

In our crowded, busy, hectic lives, dashing madly through days that follow each other with numbing frenzy, it is absolutely imperative that we escape occasionally to some private sanctuary where we can be alone with ourselves to find out who we really are. To neglect this need is to risk having sanity slip away.

Mahatma Gandhi recommended one day of total silence in every seven, since both talking and listening use nervous energy and deny the chance for meditation. A professor of theology at one of our leading universities is a bit more detailed in his advice, and he employs a different term. He says: "One of the best ways to secure spiritual serenity is to *decentralize yourself*. Forget yourself and your petty worries and fears, and think of others and how you can help them in their distress. By so doing, paradoxically, you find peace of mind."

Well, whether decentralization of self, or meditation, we need its benefits, and desperately. And if we have to take a mail-order course of instruction in how to achieve them, so be it.

Personally, when I want to be alone, with my thoughts turned inward (meditating in my own untutored fashion) I seek the help of nature. There is nothing like a walk along a woodland trail to induce spiritual tranquility. To review the catalog of hopes and dreams, refocus the aims and ambitions and rekindle the inner force that enables me to plunge ahead anew, there is no rejuvenation to match what I derive from an hour by the sea, or perched along a friendly stream, wrapped in the blanket of the night sky or tramping alone through freshly fallen snow.

I fervently hope there will never be a day on this crowded planet when I cannot slip into nature's realm for an hour or two and tell myself I'm not ever going to be caught up in the rat race again. At least not until next Wednesday.

Neighbors are people

Some wit once remarked that if you really want to know who your neighbors are, buy a set of drums and start practising.

The quip reminded me of something that happened when I was in New York City a few years ago visiting a friend, a noted concert pianist. I had dinner with him and his wife at a nearby restaurant, and then we went to their apartment.

They lived in a tall building, and the elevator, as we were going up, stopped at the seventh floor. A man stepped in, and I recognized him as a nationally famous composer. My friend knew him personally. "Paul" my friend gasped, clutching the newcomer's hand. "Of all people! I'm so glad to see you." And then in the midst of introductions and further greetings, he added: "I've been playing your *B-flat Scherzo* all over the country in recital this season. What brings you to New York?"

"What brings me to New York?" The composer laughed. "I live here, in this building, on the twentieth floor. I was just visiting someone on the seventh."

They had lived in that same apartment house for years, and didn't know it. They might as well have dwelled on opposite coasts.

There is some small excuse for this, with people who live in huge apartment complexes in big cities. But what about the rest? Do *you* take the time to get to know your neighbors? Do you know the family down the block, around the corner? Do you know the troubles and heartaches, the pleasures and joys, the dreams and aspirations of the family that lives next door? What about the man or woman you pass on the street while you're hurrying to the store, or coming home from the office—do you have a friendly smile for a greeting, or a cold, impersonal "Howdy" as you dash on? Or, worse yet, silence? No greeting at all?

We're so busy "doing our thing" these days that we seldom take time to be neighborly. We concern ourselves only with externals. We judge a man by the car he drives, the cut of his clothes, the price of his shoes.

Sad!

If we take time to probe under the surface, we find that most people are like ourselves, with problems, anxieties, fears, hopes, dreams. They're not just faces. They're real people.

If you've been denying yourself the pleasure of knowing your neighbor, get to know him next chance you have. It won't cost anything and, who knows, you might even *like* him.

If the roots are firm

Methuselah is its name.

Methuselah is a bristlecone pine, and it stands in California, said to be 4,600 years old. Officials of the Tree Research Institute in Tucson who have studied this gnarled veteran, believe it to be the oldest tree in the world. It is beginning to show its age, though, for bark covers only about 10% of its surface. It's twisted and grotesque in shape, but it has weathered the elements for centuries. It has done battle with time, yet the Institute people believe Methuselah will survive for many more centuries.

I like to think that, in some respects, people are like trees. The winds may blow, the storms may rage around us and we may grow twisted and bent as the elements hammer away at us, but if the roots are firm, if the growth is solid, we survive. If there is proper nourishment, we stand up to adversity and come out strong.

If we walk always on level ground, certain leg muscles are never used. We can strengthen them, by climbing. We all know that if our desires are handed to us on the proverbial silver platter, we never learn how to strive and seek. We all know that if we are not tested, we never measure the real strength that lies within us.

A professor at the University of Oklahoma asked a group of students to hold weights of different sorts in their hands until they grew tired. Then he repeated the experiment, only this time he gave each student a placebo, explaining that the pill contained a powerful anti-fatigue ingredient. After taking these tablets, which of course were completely without value, the students were able to double their strength.

Dr. Stewart Wolf came thus to the conclusion that most people don't know how to get the most out of the energy already at their command. A mental attitude interferes. Push that mental block aside, and who knows what can be accomplished? We all know of instances where superhuman strength comes to those facing catastrophe, but even in every day life, we can double our output by simply drawing on the energy we already have.

If the roots are firm, we survive.

Bending the barrier

In the Middle Europe of an earlier day, there was a land suffering the darkest poverty. In one community in particular, there was actual starvation, compounded by the ravages of disease. A once proud people knew destitution.

Then one day a man came to them from America. He was a Quaker, a kind, gentle person who spoke none of their language at first, and yet he was understood by all. For he brought food for those who were hungry, clothing for those who shivered with the cold. As a representative of a noble faith, he brought new hope, a new reason for living.

It can be understood why in but a short time, this man earned the profound respect and admiration and love of everyone. For he was wise, and fair. He always managed to give shoes to those whose need was greatest, not to his favorites or those who managed to become his friends; he gave without regard to the color of a man's skin, the language he spoke, or indeed to the faith he followed.

So it was a calamity almost beyond comprehension when this good man fell ill and died. Stunned, the citizens of the community could not begin to measure their loss. They could not accept the fact that he was gone, that there was nothing to do but give him burial.

Then an even more crushing circumstance became apparent. They could not bury this kind man, their great friend, in their cemetery. He was a Quaker, and the cemetery was bounded by a fence, and inside that fence the ground was consecrated and none but a Roman Catholic could be given final rest there.

What could be done?

The townspeople spoke to their Priest, but he shook his head sadly. He was powerless. It was a rule of the Church.

And so they did the only thing they could: They buried their good friend as close to the fence of that little cemetery as possible. And then they went home with heavy hearts.

But that night, the Priest went to the cemetery. He stood in silent meditation for a time, then he went to work and moved the fence. Moved it outward far enough to take in the new grave. The rule was definite enough about burial in the consecrated ground, but it said nothing about moving fences!

Alas, it is true, there all too often are fences erected around the hearts of men. But we must pray for the day when we may have the wisdom to bend those barriers, to move them altogether, to destroy them.

We must pray for the day they will be taken down, forever.

W hen *William D. Borders was installed as Arch-*
bishop of Baltimore, a considerable body of information became
known about this new prelate of the Roman Catholic Church,
including the fact that he had a personal motto. Derived from
a Papal encyclical, it was—Auscultabo ut serviam. "I will listen
that I may serve." Noble indeed, and one that we all might
adopt. It is a great gift to be able to communicate, to reach out
to others, but there are times when it is even more desirable to
remain silent, to observe, to listen, to learn. And when such
withdrawal leads to service for others, we must acknowledge
that silence can be the most pleasant of sounds.

Filters of the mind

H ave you ever listened to someone deliver a speech,
only to discuss it later with others and find they had an interpretation,
totally different from yours?

Ten people can read the same book and have ten different versions of its message. Ten people can exchange views with an eleventh and react in ten different ways to what that eleventh said.

What one may say can please half his listeners and make the other half violently angry.

How is this possible?

According to one man who thinks deeply and writes lucidly, this is the result of filter systems with which our minds are equipped, filters through which all information must pass as we are exposed to it. These filters are efficient, made up of our beliefs, our prejudices, our biases, our experiences, our certain knowledge of what is right and what is true. The information that penetrates to our minds, then, is what is left after these filters have screened out everything that might disturb our happy, one-sided view of reality.

This all sounds a bit brutal, I know, but it's true. And what's more, we all have these filters. As the hair inside the nose filters the air we breathe, so do these filters of the mind screen the thoughts and bits of information that pass through them.

The net result is that no two people are exactly alike. No two people think on precisely parallel lines. Which is why we have different religions, political parties, clashing opinions. This makes for interest and excitement and keeps things jumping in every day life, but it also harbors seeds of danger.

We are what we have become through years of living. We reflect the knowledge we have acquired, and it may be inaccurate. We hold the prejudices we have picked up along the way, and they may be damaging. We evolve into what our filter systems have permitted us to become, and those filters may be faulty.

If you keep a filter in the heating system of your home too long without cleaning it, or perhaps even replacing it, you may eventually be living in a cold home. If the filters of our minds are not occasionally cleaned, or replaced, we could be in for even more serious trouble.

It is important to remember, as philosophers have been telling us for centuries, that as we think, we are.

And it is important to remember that we will be as small as our controlling desires, as great as our dominant aspirations.

Keep those filters in good operating condition.

20-20 inner vision

In the waiting room of my ophthalmologist's office, I read a most interesting article in a British publication of recent vintage. The author was a distinguished surgeon on the staff of a London hospital. The proper magazine, and the proper place, to be sure, to read about the human eye, and eyesight. But that was not the subject of the article. It was a philosophical dissertation on what we refer to as "inner vision."

The British doctor wrote that children, obviously, enjoy a high degree of inner vision, for they fill their lives with fantasy as real as reality itself. Their imagainations have substance, and the dreams they spin acquire full dimension. But as the years flit by, we lose this priceless capacity and succumb to the realization of the world of actuality. We age, the physical eyesight dims and inner vision too loses its acuity.

We no longer see what might be, what could be, what ought to be. We see only what is.

Sadly, true. But fortunately, there are some for whom the inner eye remains sharp and keen. For some (and we must be thankful for them) this special vision never clouds. Even in the dark shadows of adversity. They always keep the ability of the child, whose gaze spans reality into beyond. They need no prescription lenses to retain this kind of sight. The optic mechanism is not involved.

When I read this magazine piece, I thought of Marja Sklodowska.

She was born in Poland on November 7, 1867. Her life began in Warsaw, with her early years filled with hardship and misery spawned by the deepest poverty. When she was but eleven years old, her mother died. Battered and shaken, she nevertheless grimly determined to push on and make something of her life, and she managed, by the age of twenty-four to go to Paris to pursue the study of medicine. Miraculously, she managed to live on thirty cents a day!

At twenty-eight, she was married. With her husband, whom she loved devotedly, she went into research, and for the first time she knew happiness, for the first time there was joy in her life. There was the promise of a bright tomorrow.

And then, while crossing a crowded street, her husband was struck by a heavy wagon. He died instantly.

Even then, this woman's inner vision did not fail her. Her dreams, her hopes, her sense of mission remained, even in the blackness of her despair. And she went on to become one of the most famous women who ever lived. Your life, and mine, have been the richer for her.

As you may suspect, this woman, whose inner vision sustained her through childhood and all the years she lived, was the one whose name, through marriage, we know as Marie Curie.

By these shores

Many years ago in a small town on the bank of a gently flowing stream, there lived a man whose body was so twisted, whose face was so disfigured, that people laughed at him and children teased him. Even dogs ran away, or barked.

And so this man left the village, where he had been born, and he went deep into the forest, where he lived alone in a hut which he built for himself. And there he found the solace he desired, the peace for which his heart cried. There he gloried in the beauty of sunrise and sunset. There he relaxed in the soft sighing of the breeze in the trees, the frolic of the creatures of the forest, the rapturous song of the birds. And the bitterness that had been in him slowly softened and began to drain away.

Then one day a visitor came into the hermit's domain. He was a tall man, and very wise, and when he was invited to spend the night, he accepted. As they sat down together to the evening meal the hermit asked the visitor to offer a prayer, but the tall man said: "No, you are the master here. It is you who must say the blessing." And so the hermit, nervous at first in the presence of the wise one, spoke his gratitude for the peace of the woods and the companionship of nature and the nourishment they were about to share. Whereupon the visitor said: "You have forgotten one thing. You have neglected to thank God for yourself."

The hermit looked away, saying nothing.

"You have been ashamed of your twisted body, your ugly face. You have retreated into the forest because you have despaired of your unattractiveness. But you have forgotten that in the eyes of God, you are as beautiful as the trees and flowers. You are as one with nature, where there is only beauty. The beauty in His eyes."

The hermit never forgot the words of the wise man, and when it happened some time later that he had the opportunity to return to the town of his birth, he moved without reluctance. And strange to say, the people of the community no longer laughed when he walked by, the children no longer teased him. He became their friend, and they his.

The twisted man with the ugly face went to the shore of the river and stood there, listening to the quiet murmur of the water, watching the shifting clouds as they prepared to enfold the setting sun. And his heart sang with joy, for he realized that he was living in the same town, with the same people. Even the same dogs. But all was different!

He was different. For he had learned to thank God, for himself.

On bended knee

The countryside was parched after endless weeks of drought and on Sunday, the minister exhorted his congregation to join him in fervent prayers for relief. On Monday, miraculously, the plea was answered. The Heavens opened and rain fell in torrents, an unceasing downpour that continued for days. By Thursday, the tiny community was all but wiped out as flood waters from the nearby stream rose, and a rescue party spied the parson sitting on the roof of his house, watching the swirling currents. "Your prayers were answered," yelled one of the rescuers. "Indeed they were," shouted the minister. "Not bad, for a little church like ours."

When do you pray? And why?

Do you turn to prayer only for fulfillment of big needs? Do you drop to your knees only when you're in trouble, when disaster threatens, only in times of drought?

Or have you discovered, as Dr. Alexis Carrell, the noted American surgeon and biologist, did, that "Prayer, like radium, is a luminous and self-generating form of energy." Perhaps you have learned the value of prayers of gratitude, prayers for no particular reason.

An executive of the American Bible Society was asked to provide a prayer that one might use at any time, a prayer "to fit any occasion." He went all the way back to Socrates for this suggestion: "Give me beauty of the inward soul, for outward beauty I am not likely to have." And then he proposed another of more recent vintage by an unknown writer: "O God, let me not turn coward before the difficulties of the day, or prove recreant to my duties. Let me not lose faith in my fellowmen. Keep me sweet and sound of heart, in spite of ingratitude, treachery or meanness. Preserve me from minding little stings, or giving them."

Does it bother you that there are those who snicker and jeer when you pray, when you expound on the power of prayer? Are you embarassed when you hear the question: "What's to pray?" If someone smirks: "What for? To whom?"

I suggest you pray for *them*. They need it.

John Wanamaker, one of this country's greatest merchants, was asked: "What was your most glorious hour?" Wanamaker replied, not when he concluded his most successful business deal, but: "It was when I was a child and my mother took my baby hands and folded them in prayer as she pointed me to God."

May I offer one more prayer for no particular occasion. It asks merely for serenity of the soul:

"Slow me down, Lord. Ease the pounding of my heart by the quieting of my mind. Steady my hurried pace with the vision of the eternal reach of time. Give me, amid the confusion of my day, the calmness of the everlasting hills. Inspire me to send my roots deep into the soil of life's endearing values, that I may grow toward the stars of my greater destiny."

To improve your face

Users of the English language have a reservoir of roughly 600,000 words to choose from when they wish to communicate. Of these, we are told, the average person knows, and uses, a mere handful, perhaps seven or eight hundred. Which explains why so much of common speech is dull and colorless.

But have you ever thought how many ways there are to communicate, both positively and negatively, without words? By gestures only? A raised eyebrow, a shoulder shrug, a flick of the finger can often speak volumes. Studies have been made that indicate humans are capable of approximately 70,000 different facial expressions and body movements, each of which is equal to making a statement.

While sailing down the Rhine during a visit to Germany, I found myself with a family that I supposed to be native, and I was prepared to exercise my limited knowledge of their language. I discovered they were from Yugoslavia, and of their tongue I knew not a single word, and they understood as much English. Despite that barrier, I spent two delightful hours with them, and I would guess between us we tackled most of those 70,000 gestures. But I can tell you, the system worked. We did communicate!

The use of gesture-language, however, is not limited to foreigners who do not understand the spoken word anyway. It is frequently employed, and often eloquently, between friends. It may be a supplement to speech, or stand alone.

Take the common act of holding out the hand to shake that of another. In our culture, a beautiful movement that requires no accompanying words. It is complete in itself. Then there is the even more magnificent gesture we make when we extend both hands to help someone, to offer support, to lift the fallen. And what we might call the gesture of understanding, a pat on the back, an arm around the shoulder, a gentle touch on the arm.

Now it must be said that in thus communicating with people of widely differing cultures, there may be problems. For the gestures could have widely differing meanings. This is particularly true of Western and Eastern lands. But there is one, the simplest and most effective of all, which may be brought into play anywhere in the world without possibility of misunderstanding. I refer to—the smile!

My travels have taken me to many countries around the globe, and I have struggled to communicate with and without knowledge of the native tongues, and the smile has never failed me. It means the same everywhere. It is understood by young and old, men and women. It is magical. It creates miracles. I don't know how many of the 70,000 gestures may be in your arsenal, but that one is a must! If you haven't found out how much you can accomplish with a smile, wait no longer. Try it! A smile speaks volumes. Besides (check this in a mirror) it'll improve your face.

Big deal!

Has some long-forgotten uncle suddenly passed away, leaving you his entire estate, including art treasures and oil wells? Did you buy a fifty cent lottery ticket and wind up a millionare? Did you wake up this morning to learn that by acclamation the citizenry, aware of your eminence at last, had elected you President of the United States? No? Nothing so big has happened to you?

It hasn't happened to me, either.

But as I write these words, a blazing red cardinal is perched on the branch of a tree outside my window, cheeping his annoyance that I have not yet provided his daily ration of sunflower seeds. And I'm glad he's reminding me, because it is a great joy to watch him, and his mate, as I do every day. They provide regular pleasure and satisfaction.

What's the connection?

Years ago, I used to go for walks in the country, following an old, dusty road that led past a ramshackle farm. I hiked that way so often I learned to know a farmer who lived along that road, and sometimes I'd sit on the porch of his battered house and he'd tell me about his life. He always seemed supremely contented and cheerful. He owned few of the world's goods, but that never troubled him. In spring and summer there were always flowers blooming around that house, his wife was usually inside singing, and even his dog wore a perpetually jovial expression. "I take pleasure in little things," he said one day. "There are so many of them."

What a philosophy!

You're seeking inner serenity in a world that threatens to make you come apart at the seams? You say you've had a successful life but there's something missing and it just might be happiness? Let's face it. It's not very likely that the old violin you found in the attic (the one Junior used to play when he was taking lessons) will turn out to be a genuine Stradivarius worth a king's ransom, but life is full of glorious little joys and beauties on all sides. They surround you now. Savor *them!*

May I oversimplify?

I love to travel, always have. Come to my home some time and start me talking about the trips I've taken, ask me to show you things. Chances are the first items I'll pick up will be a handful of basically worthless stones I found along the coast of Maine. Or a starfish, properly preserved and varnished, that I plucked from the gleaming white sand on the beach of a tiny Caribbean island. Or a small rusty cannonball I found in the ruins of a fortress in Haiti. Or—

Come to think of it, that's not oversimplification. Life is made up of "little things." Look for them. Cherish them. You'll find they generate *big* happiness.

Welcome the inevitable

In August of 1975, in Florence, Italy, I stood before the tomb of a great man. Galileo Galilei. And I remembered that it was in the year 1633 that this giant was summoned to Rome, there to appear before the Inquisition, where he was tried, found guilty of heresy and sentenced to prison. His crime? This supreme physicist and astronomer had learned through scientific experiment that the Earth and the planets moved around the sun, and the sun was the center of our'solar system. He had said this publicly, and had written it. This was contrary to the established beliefs of the time, and Galileo was therefore in deep trouble. "I can prove I am right," he said. "I can convince you. Look through my telescope!" But the men in power refused to look. They were convinced that the earth itself was the center of the Universe and no evidence could convince them to the contrary. Galileo was condemned.

In any age, including ours today, there are men as blind and obdurate as those of the Inquisition. They are convinced that their stand is right, they refuse to "look through the telescope" at truth, they are content and satisfied with things as they are and will accept no evidence to budge them from their positions of stability and security. They are not conditioned to change.

Change!

That's the key word. I know a man who eats the same thing for breakfast every day of the week but Sunday. His lunch never varies either. Same thing, day after day. Year after year. He's a dear friend and we've argued the matter countless times. He's comfortable with monotony. It would drive me clean out of my skull.

There are people who feel secure by doing things as they've always done them, by surrounding themselves with the familiar, the customary, the traditional. They instinctively distrust and dislike all that's new and different, everything that departs from the "old shoe" comfort of the past. They fight change. It's a losing battle, and always is, but they go on fighting.

The wise man lives life so that he can accept change, sway with it. This can begin with something so simple as *not* always eating the same food, *not* always dining in the same restaurant, *not* always driving through the same streets on the way to work in the morning. Court change, seek variety. The world is too full of wonderful things to hold to the same pattern day after day. So much is missed. Furthermore, change is inevitable. History tells us that. Surveys show that those who resist change are swept aside as the years flow by. The tide billows on. Those who swim with it survive. Those who don't, drown.

Who said it? I've forgotten, but he said it eloquently:

"God grant me the courage to change what can be changed, and the peace of mind to accept things I cannot change, and the wisdom to know the difference."

The horseless carriage

W e're making progress.
The old, narrow roads where two cars could barely pass, now have been replaced by superhighways and turnpikes where six, ten, sometimes more, cars can all crash at once.

Often, when I'm stalled somewhere in heavy traffic, breathing somebody else's gaseous exhaust fumes, knowing my blood pressure is rising, I amuse myself thinking about how it used to be. I wasn't living then, mind you, but I've read all about it.

I know there are places today (Bermuda, for example) where the speed limit is 20 miles per hour, tops, but can you believe that right here in the U. S. of A., you were, generally, allowed to drive at 10 mph in the open country, 5 in the cities, no more? And if, around the year 1900, a policeman apprehended a driver for speeding, he very likely did so pedaling a bicycle because bikes were faster than cars?

There were around two million miles of road in this country then, but only 150 were paved. And if you went roaring down the bumps at 5 mph and you met a horse, you were required to stop, turn off your motor and wait till the horse was safely past.

There was a hilarious rule in England that said each automobile had to be preceded by a man waving a red flag, while here (in Vermont) by law, a man walked in front of every auto carrying a red lantern.

These days when I venture onto a superhighway, accelerating like crazy to avoid being crushed from behind by drivers who are bent on reaching their destination or the nearest cemetery, whichever comes first, in the shortest possible time, I find myself chuckling over the knowledge that in Dover, New Hampshire, where the local speed limit was 8 mph, police frequently stopped reckless motorists by stretching a rope across the highway. And outside another New England town, there once was a sign that read: "The Speed Limit This Year Is Secret. Violators Will Be Fined $10.00."

Autos weren't very popular in those days. They were hated with passion by farmers, who delighted in giving atrociously wrong directions to stranded motorists. And in the cities, people used to express their displeasure with the horseless carriage by sprinkling tacks, nails and broken bottles in the streets. You had to buy gas at paint or hardware stores, and for overnight parking you had to use a livery stable, provided the owner and the horses didn't object.

But apparently thieves were at work, even then. I understand Henry Ford himself used to guard against crime by chaining his car to a lamp post!

Is this your best?

Do you happen to own a Picasso? A Bracque, perhaps, or a Miro? Maybe your tastes run to Rembrandt, Cassatt, Van Gogh?

Listen, I'm kidding—

But the next time you look at a painting, or even a reproduction, study it, search, and probably down in the right hand corner you will find the artist's identification, very likely his or her signature. By signing it, the creator of the work is saying: "This is mine. This represents the best I could do at the time. I did it!"

How many of us could do the same?

We aren't, to be sure, all artists. Some of us don't even produce tangibles, like paintings. Nevertheless, the question holds: Could we sign our work? Could we claim it as ours, representing our best effort? Could we say, without shame, I did this?

How many times have you bought something, an appliance, a new car, clothing, only to take it home and have it fail to live up to its advertised standards? How many times have you complained about shoddy merchandise? How many times have you moaned about disappearing values in a world where workers are ever more interested in quantity and not quality?

A more critical question: Are you one of these?

I remember a quote from the great Leonardo da Vinci: "Thou, O God, dost sell us all good things, at the price of Labor."

It seems more important to quit on time, to work as short a week as possible, to earn the highest dollar, than to pay the price of labor, than to give one's best effort. Pride of workmanship is vanishing. Quality is becoming merely a word.

It is not enough to see these faults in others; this attitude must be attacked within ourselves. Attacked and destroyed. Or it will destroy us.

I remind you of the woman who approached a noted pianist after a concert and said: "I'd give half my life to play as you do." To which the artist replied: "That, Madam, is what it cost me."

The price of labor.

An American tourist visited the Black Forest region of Germany and watched a man painstakingly carving the casing for one of the cuckoo clocks made there. Noting the slow rate of progress, the tourist said: "My good man, you'll never make any money that way."

"Sir," was the reply, "I'm not making money, I'm making cuckoo clocks."

Gratitude

I n March, 1975, Clarence L. Munn died. "Biggie" Munn was hired as the football coach of Michigan State University in 1947 when the school's team was foundering, and in his first game, his Spartans were smashed 55–0 by the opposition. In subsequent years his players rallied, and "Biggie" established a record of 54 wins, nine losses and two ties.

My lack of interest in football verges on the spectacular, so it is logical to ask: What cooks?

This!

Michigan State played in the Rose Bowl and won. When all his triumphant players had piled into the dressing room after that rowdy victory, "Biggie" blew his whistle and asked for silence. Choking with emotion he said: "I've never been so proud of a team in my life. I want to thank all of you. There are tears in my eyes, but I can't help it. I appreciate it so much, let's—let's say a prayer."

And the Michigan State football players went down on their knees, and Biggie Munn's eyes were not the only ones glistening with tears.

"God bless you," he said as the prayer ended.

Now there was a man! He called for a prayer *in gratitude!*

When we're in trouble, when we need help, when we're slammed around by fate and the going is rough, some of us remember to pray for strength, for assistance. When illness comes or the breaks go against us and the clouds are dark, some remember to seek divine intervention. But when all goes well, when the sun shines again, when our prayers are answered, how many of us are thoughtful enough to say another prayer of thanks?

A little item in a newspaper is glued to my memory. Some years ago the Postmaster General, one January, spoke of the avalanche of letters to Santa Claus that flood the nation's mails every December. Millions of children, begging the jolly man to bring them presents. But after Christmas, there is traditionally a mere trickle of mail to Santa. A few, a very few, remember to express their gratitude.

A well known atheist suffered a serious fall on the icy streets of Baltimore one winter, and two passersby went to her assistance and took her home. She neglected to ask their names, so she wrote a letter to the Editor of the morning newspaper to thank them for their kindness.

How many who are not atheists are as thoughtful about expressing gratitude for assistance given? The Good Samaritan doesn't always come when we call, but when he does, are we properly grateful?

Now you see why I thought so much of "Biggie" Munn.

To trim the ego

O ne time, in the not too long ago, I sailed on a freighter bound for the West Indies. She was of modest size, this ship, about fifteen thousand gross tons, but she looked huge when I arrived at the dock to go aboard. Her prow towered above me and I knew that on this voyage I would be secure. Come what may, she would be a sturdy home for the next several weeks.

Ahead, lay palm-fringed islands, white sand beaches gleaming in unending sun, exotic ports with strange and exciting happenings, people speaking in foreign tongues, cargo to be discharged and loaded, a fascinating parade of new experiences day after day.

And all this, in due course, came to pass.

But, before, in the South Atlantic, we sailed into the outer fringe of a hurricane, and something unexpected occurred. A vital part of the vessel's mechanism, deep below, ceased to function, and at eight o'clock one evening, all forward motion stopped. Till dawn the next morning we pitched and rolled and tossed like a matchstick at the mercy of the heaving sea, as men struggled below decks to repair the damage.

I do not get seasick, ever, so I went topside, to stand in a protected spot on the upper deck just below the bridge. It was a frightening thing to watch those gigantic waves wash over us, to sense the awesome power of the sea, to be so helpless. Our fifteen thousand tons seemed insignificant, then. I never felt so small in my life. I never felt so completely, so unspeakably and utterly unimportant.

Later, when we resumed our journey and the ship sailed lazily through the calm Caribbean, I lay, one night, on a forward hatch, staring up into the black velvet of the sky. There were stars we never see, up North. And they were so big, so bright these distant suns—that I felt with small effort I might touch them. And then, I felt even smaller. A mere speck on the deck of a tiny ship sailing on a huge sea spinning on the Planet Earth suspended in the vastness of Eternity!

I asked myself: what am I?

There are times when I get to thinking that maybe I am somebody. In an unguarded moment, I may feel that in the overall scheme of things, I have a role to play and dammit, it's time that all men should know!

And then, I remember.

I remember that storm at sea, and that crippled vessel bobbing like a child's toy swirling in a gutter flooded after a summer rain, and the majestic panoply of the night sky totally beyond comprehension. I remember, and instantly my ego is whittled down to size.

That was a voyage to remember.

There is a way out

It has been said that everyone is honest, up to a certain point. How about you? To what point does your honesty extend?

George Washington once remarked: "Few men have the virtue to withstand the highest bidder." How high must the bids go before your resolve crumbles?

Here's an interesting story:

A father and son were walking down the street of a large city when they found a man's glove on the sidewalk. The man explained that since it obviously belonged to someone else, the proper thing to do was to place it on the railing of a nearby building so that the owner, should he come looking for it, might regain his property. But then, a bit further on, the two discovered a second glove, clearly the mate of the first. The father tried it on, found it to be a perfect fit, and exclaimed: "Jimmy, my boy, run back and fetch me the other. I have just acquired a new pair of gloves!"

Now then, about your honesty. Does it extend to one glove, or both? Can you be trusted up to a certain point, or all the way?

It often requires great strength of character to be honest all the way. It frequently calls for more guts than lying.

You need no formal education to learn the difference between right and wrong. You don't need to have a string of academic degrees tacked after your name to know what is the honest thing to do. The issues may be clouded, varying pressures may be brought to bear, temptation may loom, but the right course of action is always clear. There is no twilight zone. We know what is right. The question is: do we have the strength, the character?

There is always a way out!

There is a very famous painting, done by a noted artist. The canvas depicts the Devil, seated at a chess board with a young man. The Devil has just made his move, and his opponent's Queen is checkmated. The young man's face shows defeat, it is stained with despair. The painting is so well done that those who understand the game of chess look at it, study the board, and instantly feel sympathetic for the young man because they realize he's finished. He has come to a blind alley and there is no way out.

But one day Paul Murphy, one of the great chess players, went to the art gallery to see this painting. He was fascinated by it. He stood in silence for a long time studying the chess board, and then, unmindful of those around him, he addressed the painted players: "You still have a move!" He pointed to the young man on the canvas. "Don't give up! You still have a move!"

For the man who is honest, all the way, there is always a way out.

There once was a man so despondent, so wracked by care and worry, that he decided to end it all. There was no point in living, so he started to walk across the city to a bridge he knew, the bridge from which we would jump. However, as he walked, he made a decision: If, on the way, he met someone, anyone, with a friendly, smiling disposition, somebody who by his manner could bring a ray of cheer into his life, he would turn back. End of story. We don't know whether he jumped or not. But there is a question: If, while walking toward that bridge, he had met you, would you have given him the courage to turn back and try again? Would you?

The twists of fate

Sometime, when you haven't anything else to do, think back over you life to the times when things went wrong, yet came out right.

I'm referring to the picnic that was washed out by rain so you stayed home and had a good time anyway. Or when your vacation plans collapsed so you went somewhere else and thus met the man, or woman, you eventually married. Or the job you applied for and didn't get, and now you're happy because you found something even better and got started in a new line of work, and are happy and successful.

And I'm referring to the twists and turns of fate that happen with startling frequency. For example, the young Navy officer who was about to leave for sea duty when he was informed of illness in his family. So he went home to be with his ailing wife and his ship left without him. Fate kept him from sailing on the last, the fatal voyage, of the American submarine, Thresher.

And I'm thinking of a friend of mine who was in a minor automobile accident on the way to the airport. She missed her plane. Fate prevented her from being on board an air liner that went down, with no survivors.

There is another such episode. Epic, you might call it.

A few years ago I visited the island of Martinique in the French West Indies. A beautiful place of glorious white beaches washed by the blue waters of the Caribbean, high mountains rising majestically from the lush green of the tropics, graceful palm trees waving in the gentle trade winds. And an incredible history!

I told my guide where I wanted to go, and he knew why. We had to speak in French for he knew no English, but my rusty tongue didn't interfere. I knew the story before he told it to me. We drove up, up to the thin, cool air of the city of St. Pierre. It seemed sleepy, slow-moving. I saw the people, the little stores, men and women working in the fields, the old cathedral. And the jail.

The jail!

I looked up from the streets of St. Pierre, and when the clouds occasionally parted, I saw it. The jutting peak that was Mt. Pelee. It was easy for me to imagine that I was back in the year 1902. Mt. Pelee is a volcano, and on May 8th, it blew. The violent eruption is known as one of the most devastating of history's natural catastrophies. Death came to 40,000 in a rain from the sky. And when rescue teams finally dug through the rubble, one survivor was found. One! By a staggering twist of fate, one man lived through that awful hell. And he was the sole occupant of the deep underground prison in the city of St. Pierre.

Green elbows

It was a really handsome garden, full of healthy looking plants, bursting with incipient vegetables. I congratulated him, said I was submerged in envy. "Nothing to it," he said. "I planted the seeds indoors early in spring, watered them, gave them light, thinned them, then transplanted the seedlings to a cold frame. Then in early May I threw the whole mess in the trash and bought these plants at a nursery."

Nature is fiendish.

Every fall it happens. I'll be reading a book, say, when I hear this strange noise, and I go outside and look up and there they are. Flocks of geese flying past the full moon on their way south. Some inner mechanism tells them it's time to head for warmer climes, the way certain animals know the moment has come to go into hibernation, the way tiny little plants realize the day has arrived to poke their heads above ground in spring, the way it tells my garden how to schedule itself so that every blasted edible will come to the peak of perfection at the exact time I go on vacation!

It never fails.

Take last year. I planted everything early. Tomatoes, corn, peppers, carrots, raddishes, squash, beans. The works. Early because the year before my garden popped its goodies while I was in Europe, and I'd planted late. So I defied the frosts and got away with it. I did everything right. We had a good spring, plenty of rain, lots of sun. The garden was lush. A neighbor said I obviously had green thumbs up to my elbows.

What happened?

Nature found out when I planned to be away, re-programmed the whole growing schedule, and those who hold the key to my garden enjoyed delicious red tomatoes and fat green peppers and crisp raddishes and tasty squash while I was mending the tissues frayed by work on the island of Antigua in the Caribbean.

I can't win.

I've tried subterfuge. One year I told nobody of my travel plans. I was especially careful not to breathe a word anywhere near my garden. It didn't work. My friends and neighbors enjoyed my harvest that year, too.

I've even consulted experts. A friend who is president of her garden club said she could throw no light on the problem, suggested we'd just have to chalk it up as one of the mysteries of nature. I hate to admit defeat. I enjoy a challenge, but after years of trying, I'm afraid I'll have to confess that this one stumps me. I see no way out of the dilemma except to schedule my holidays in winter.

A minority of one

One night, many years ago, a ship was plowing through the calm seas on a voyage to the East. Below decks, a passenger lay ill in his cabin, when suddenly he heard the cry: "Man overboard!"

A member of the crew had somehow fallen into the water. The passenger was too sick to go above to lend a helping hand, so he did the only thing he could. He took his cabin lamp and held it close to the porthole so that its rays might shine out on the sea. Shortly afterward, the passenger learned that the crewman had been saved. And the next morning, he learned the full story. It had been *his* feeble effort that had brought about the seaman's rescue. The rays from his lamp had enabled others to locate the drowning sailor.

The light from one small lamp!

As I read, and turn, the pages of history, I never cease to marvel at the countless illustrations of the *power of one man*. The good he can achieve, if he makes the effort. The miracles he can accomplish, if he but tries.

Each of us, at some time or other, is a minority. We are all pioneers, standing alone, now and then.

Every man or woman with a new idea is a minority, often struggling against violent opposition. Every achiever is first a pioneer, perhaps a radical. Every hero who has walked across the chronicle of man's endeavor has been first, a rebel.

There is scarcely a force equal to that of a creative minority. The world has always moved forward through the efforts of a few. In science, medicine, literature, the arts, any field—there is always the handful of names that glow with the radiance of the pioneer.

In going through an old copy of the *Newsletter On Intellectual Freedom*, I found this statement by John Gough: "There is not a social, political or religious privilege that was not bought for us by the blood and tears and patient suffering of the minority. It is the minority that has stood in the front of every moral conflict, and achieved all that is noble in the history of the world."

Brother

I know a most remarkable lady. Whether you are meeting her for the first time, or greeting her as an old friend, she addresses you as "brother." And when she speaks the word, a glow spreads over you, a warmth that defies description. She has devoted her life to the cause of brotherhood, she has given her most forceful effort to prove that all men are indeed brothers. And under her influence, you know it is true.

After a visit to this wonderful old friend, I picked up again Brooks Atkinson's book, "Once Around The Sun," and reread a portion that impressed me so deeply when it was first published. Atkinson, for many years the drama critic of The New York Times, wrote that he considered "brother" to be the most sublime word in the English language. To him, the word denotes love and respect freely given and without obligation; it carries with it qualities of loyalty and esteem, bonds that are deep and understanding that's profound.

He concludes by observing that the finest world imaginable is that world in which the brotherhood of man reigns, and that when *all* men are truly brother, and not before, the golden age will begin.

Perhaps this is why, when this dear friend calls me "brother" I am so pleased and touched. It seems for a fleeting moment I am glimpsing Atkinson's golden age. I am in the presence of someone whose life has been a sermon on brotherhood.

To her, we are all embarked on the same journey, perhaps by different paths, perhaps by separate roads, but toward a common destination. As she sees it, our struggles on the way will be diminished as soon as we are wise enough to understand and respect each other, to love one another, to lean on our brother's shoulder, to grasp his hand, to offer support without hesitation to all.

I shall be everlastingly grateful to the design of fate that brought me within her orbit so early in my life. She had so much to do with shaping my own psyche and philosophy.

I shall never forget a story this friend told me. It took place on a cold, wintry day in New York City, many years ago. Sleet was falling and walking was difficult in the vicinity of 42nd Street. People were rushing in all directions as best they could, and a young black man struggled to keep from falling, a heavy valise in one hand, a huge suitcase in the other. A strong hand suddenly appeared at his side—a white hand—to seize the valise. A cheerful, pleasant voice said: "Let me take that, brother. The weather's too bad for such heavy bundles."

The one protested, the other insisted. "I'm going your way," he said. And so they walked together to Grand Central Station, chatting like old friends.

The one man was Theodore Roosevelt. The other was the great educator—Booker T. Washington.

Power and glory

Rudyard Kipling once addressed the graduating class at McGill University, his theme: if a man's scale of values is based solely on material wealth, he will be in difficulty all his life. He advised his hearers not to pay too much attention to fame, power and money. "Some day you will meet a man who cares for none of these," he said, "and then you will know how poor you are."

Kipling spoke true.

A lady told me she found the most difficult task facing her as a parent, was that of instilling a workable sense of values in her children. The dollar, deflated, inflated, or otherwise, is god, even for the very young, and destroying that theory and replacing it with another that "works" is not easy.

I told her a story:

A woman lived in a rural area and raised chickens, more or less as a hobby. One day as she was shelling corn for her flock, she noticed that a valuable pearl was missing from a ring on her finger. Heartsick, she knew the gem must be somewhere in the corn, but she couldn't find it. She searched, knowing that to locate it would be like finding the proverbial needle in a haystack, nevertheless, each day as she poured corn for her chickens, she maintained her sharp watch. And one morning there it was! In the trough along with corn and small pebbles, there was her pearl!

That pearl, worth fifty times all the chickens, was as valueless to them as any common stone.

In large measure, we determine our own sense of values. It is not easy, when sports figures sign multi-million dollar contracts and all the world hears. It's tough to do when those who contribute little or nothing to man's welfare take home salaries ten or twenty times those of men and women who weave the very fabric of our well being. Yet it must be done. Wrapped in a philosophy that encompasses appreciation of basic values, we can insulate ourselves against jealousy, insecurity, dissatisfaction and unhappiness.

I have another story that may help:

A nobleman was showing a visitor through his palace. They came to a guarded chamber in which reposed a collection of exquisite stones. Diamonds, rubies, opals. It was impossible, said the nobleman, to calculate their value. "Yet," he added sadly, "they yield no income."

"I have only two stones," said the visitor. "They cost a mere five dollars each, and they yield a comfortable income." And so he took the nobleman down the hillside to the mill which he owned, and showed him two grinding mill stones.

What did you say?

Y ou have, I'm sure, walked through crowds and picked up stray odds and ends of conversation, bits of talk that flow into and out of earshot. Usually these fragments mean nothing, sometimes they are amusing, now and then you catch the whole message.

One of the latter occurred, for me, in a crowded elevator. I heard one woman, speaking in low tones to another, say: "I'm sure he's a brilliant man, but I've never understood anything he's said to me in all the years I've known him." As we reached the lobby and dispersed, I caught the punch line: "He just can't communicate."

The lady was mentioning a problem that is unfortunately widespread. How many times have you heard a speaker who is a leader in his field, yet what he says is dull? How many times have you been exposed to experts who were unable to verbalize their expertise? One thinks of the tree in the forest: If there's nobody to hear, is there a sound? If you are learned in your field, whatever it may be, how much good is it if you cannot communicate?

There are those skilled in the business of overcoming this problem, men and women trained to train others in the art of communicating. I am not one of them. But I do have a few suggestions that may be of value.

For one, if I could write this article in Greek, I would not do so, for the obvious reason that I would severely restrict my readers. Over simplification? Perhaps, but that is what many do, in essence. They cannot focus the level of their communication in such a way that they may be understood by the largest number. They speak, or write, on a lofty level beyond the grasp of the audience. They employ the lexicon of their field, leaving behind all those who are not trained to understand.

You must learn to put yourself in the position of the other man, and then communicate at his level. This is not "talking down," a detestable practise, but rather seeking a common level of understanding. You must really like people to be able to do this, perhaps you must love them.

You must *care* about reaching others. You must *want* to touch them. You must *try* to enter their minds, and hearts.

I offer this not only to the man who addresses a multitude, but for the one-to-one situation as well.

We have developed the tool for communication. We call it language. And this, of course, is one reason why words are so vital. The tool is flexible, of almost endless variety, endowed with infinite gradations of power. We need to use it properly. If we fail to do so, we cannot communicate.

The last analysis

The snow was deep.

When it began falling, it was moist, heavy. It clung to everything. Then as it deepened, the termperature dropped and the winds came. Power lines went down. Telephone wires broke under the stress. Roads were blocked. The plows couldn't chew their way through the drifting mounds of white. Little or no traffic moved, and eventually the city came to a halt. The whole community was swallowed in the choking blanket.

Remember it?

There have been several such storms throughout my years, but the one to which I refer paralysed the eartern states some years ago. Even the largest cities couldn't function.

Such storms, I know, mean hardship and suffering to many, and for this I am sorry. But to most, they bring periods of isolation wherein normal activity ceases and people find they are alone with themselves. They are, whether they like it or not, thrown upon their own resources, customary attractions and distractions of every-day life are suspended. No one wants to bring on hardship and suffering, but since we do not call the shots I can say it's good to have this sort of thing happen now and again. In the stillness, the vacuum, we find ourselves taking stock, reviewing our sense of values, brought closer to our neighbors and ourselves.

We've all seen it happen.

Even a severe summer storm can do it. When the power lines come down, or a transformer somewhere fails and we huddle together with our flickering candles. Even such an experience, which may last only a brief time, tells us something of who we are, and why. Those who have lived through the horrors of a hurricane, or a storm at sea, will know what I mean. The experience may be terrifying at the time, but it can hardly fail to be ennobling. At the least, it brings us down a peg or two. It serves to remind us that we are not supreme, that nature must indeed be reckoned with, and that we are much more interdependent than we sometimes realize.

And it reminds us that there is a force, a power—call it what you will—totally beyond self.

I remember a man who was not content to wait for nature to engulf him in the isolation of a storm. Richard E. Byrd. He courted that isolation by going into the frozen vastness of the Antarctic to undertake scientific research. But I am wondering if Admiral Byrd was not responding to something deep within himself when he made his long journeys into perpetual ice and snow. Did he not, in the Antarctic, know and understand himself more fully than anywhere else? One time, from the frozen wastes, he wrote a long, philosophical letter to a friend, and he ended with these words: "Man's problem, in the last analysis, is man himself."

Only this endures

Some years ago I was browsing around in one of my favorite bookstores. It was in Philadelphia, and I struck up a conversation with another customer, an elderly and very disheveled man, poorly dressed, dirty and unkempt. You would look at him and know in an instant that he had taken a lot of lumps in his life. Yet, I found him strangely fascinating. He used impeccable English and he wore an aura of dignity. I could not then, and I cannot now, find any other word for it but—character. However, storm-ravaged the exterior, something of indelible character radiated from the man.

When I went to the rear of the shop to pay for my selections I asked the cashier if she knew who this unfortunate soul was, and I learned that he was indeed somebody. He had been a professor at the University of Pennsylvania some years before (biochemistry, I think it was) and one tragedy after another had beset him until, at length, he cracked. He was sent to a mental institution. After long incarceration, he emerged, but he never regained his footing. He continued to live alone, tragically forlorn, pathetically out of tune with the world.

I often think of that man, even today, and of the way his character shone through the dirt and grime and litter of his life. He had lost everything else, but not the hard core of the inner self that once was his. No, that still *was* his. I think of him especially when I meet someone who is all spit and polish and bright and shining and—empty.

What, precisely, is character? I don't know who said it, but this is hard to beat: "Character is what you are, in the dark."

Character is what you are when nobody is looking, when you are not seeking praise, when you are not concerned about whether you have an audience, when you don't care who gets the credit. Character is what you are, inside. Somehow, I'm sure that my ragged old man in Philadelphia had met that test.

When I think of him, I remember something written by O. S. Marsden. I copied it, years ago:

"There are silent depths in the ocean which the storms that lash the surface into fury, never reach. There are people who have learned not to live on the surface of their being, but who reach down into the depths where, in the stillness, the voice of God is heard, where they absorb the great principles of life and are not affected by the thousands of storms and tempests which cause so much suffering and unhappiness and mar so many lives. In the depths of their being they find the Divine stabilizing power which carries them poised and serene, even through a hurricane of difficulties."

I rather think Horace Greeley was right. He said: "Fame is a vapor, popularity is an accident, and riches take wings. Only one thing endures—character."

Fear of failure

Show me the man," Albert Einstein once said, "who does not know the meaning of the word 'fail' and I will show you a man who ought to buy a dictionary."

There must be few, indeed, who started up the ladder of success and who reached the top without ever slipping, stumbling, falling back now and again. It is rarely an easy climb.

Now this is a subject about which so much has been written by so many, that *any* words of mine are of necessity trite. Still I think we need to be reminded, ocassionaly, that failure must be classified as an almost vital ingredient of success. I think we need to tell ourselves, at least once a year, that though we remember Babe Ruth for hitting 714 home runs, he did strike out 1,330 times. We need to recall Cy Young, another baseball great, who won 511 victories during his career but whose records also list nearly twice as many losses.

At Fort Necessity, during the French and Indian War, there was a young American officer who capitulated to the enemy, but we don't revere George Washington for this moment of failure.

Take the word itself:

F—Fickleness
A—Affectation
I —Indifference
L—Laziness
U—Uppishness
R—Recklessness
E—Envy

Sure, they contribute to Failure. But there's another word, not included in that list. Fear. Terribly important! It must be cataloged. Many are so afraid of the possibility of failing that they take no action at all. The fear of coming a cropper prevents many from trying. For fear of missing the mark, they never take aim.

The strong, stumble, and try again. The determined fall, then dust themselves off and make a new beginning. The ambitious slip, then mend their cuts and bruises and climb anew.

Look at the career of this one man:

His business failed in 1831. He went into politics and was defeated in his run for the state legislature in 1832. He failed in business again in 1833. In 1835 his sweetheart died, and in 1836 he had a nervous breakdown. He tried for Speaker of the House in 1838, and failed. He tried for Elector in 1840 and was defeated. He tried for Congress in 1843 and failed. He tried for Congress in 1848, and failed. He failed in his try for the Senate in 1855, and in his campaign for Vice President in 1856. And he failed again when he tried for the Senate in 1858.

But we remember Abraham Lincoln because he became President of the United States in 1860. There are many, this writer among them, who consider him one of the greatest men who ever lived. He had no fear of failure.

A friend, thin of thatch, allowed as how he would visit the nearest wig-maker and order up a new sky piece but for one basic problem. "Would my friends recognize me? How would I face the public for the first time?" As a public service, I offer this suggestion to all who hesitate to wear a wig: Grow a moustache. Possibly even a beard. Allow this hirsute adornment to develop slowly till the point where it is downright bushy. Then suddenly shave off the whole mess, slap on your wig, and go out into the light of day. Your friends will gasp. "I see you've shaved off your beard!" They won't even notice your new hair. Obviously, this works only for men. When I have a plan built for women, I'll issue proper bulletins.

And these were dreams

The dream of yesterday is the hope of today and the reality of tomorrow.

An Egyptian king once dreamed, and the Pyramids of Cheops rose on desert sands. The dream of another ancient turned into stone and the awesome Sphinx sits in eternal silence near the Nile.

A man named Columbus dreamed, and white-sailed ships crossed uncharted seas. Michaelangelo dreamed, and cold, sleeping marble assumed warm beauty. Men named Hudson and Fulton dreamed, and mechanical monsters moved over and under the water. The Pilgrims dreamed, and found shores where men might discover new frontiers. Marquette and Lewis and Clark dreamed many dreams, and the bones of oxen, men and women and children, formed a bridge to span a land now crossed by bright-hulled airships in speeding moments.

Morse, Marconi, Edison, Bell—they, and others like them, dreamed wild dreams, and though there were many who did not understand, who laughed and jeered, they forced their vision into being. They forged their dreams into reality.

Others dreamed, and a new land was born, chiseled from the hard, uncompromising wilderness of a vast continent, seeking liberty, seeking freedom, seeking justice. In later days, men dreamed and automobiles appeared, and highways, and trains. Then there were those who dreamed, and men hurtled through the fearsome void of space, to walk on the barren reaches of the moon.

Within memory, a black man stood before a memorial in Washington and spoke to the multitude of his dream, a dream that all men might join in wisdom to realize their common destiny.

And another in Washington, who also fell to an assassin's bullet, spoke one day in eloquence: "Some men see things as they are and say, why? I dream of things that never were, and say, why not?"

So long as man can dream, nothing is impossible.

The dreams of today, become the stone and steel of tomorrow. It has always been so, it will always be so. The process has not stopped. There are times for dreaming, times for doing.

They are linked. The one becomes the other.

There are those who dream, today. In isolated pockets of the world men and women who respond to an inner vision. We need to join them. We need to turn our faces to the future, unafraid, unshaken by doubts, untouched by fear. We may not see the goal, but it is there. Our vision may be clouded, but no matter.

We need to dream toward the day when man may be fully alive to his own heritage. We need to dream of that glorious day when we shall all know—Peace!

The glacier of neglect

In 1955, it was reported that Fernando Navarra and his eleven year old son Raphael, climbed formidable Mt. Ararat and discovered an estimated fifity tons of wooden debris under the ice of the mountain's glacier. Navarra insisted that the shape of the Ark was still discernible, that of a large ship about 450 feet long. Many of the scientific community rejected the find, but colleagues in Paris and Madrid studied wood samples and set their age at about 5,000 years.

Whether or not remnants of the Ark still exist beneath the glacier at a depth of about 13,000 feet, as some insist, it would seem that man too is in some ways in a frozen predicament. His spiritual side is buried under a mountain of non-concern, hidden by a glacier of neglect.

We know that even in those countries where non-religion is the official government posture, the spiritual fervor of the people still burns. And here in our country, though it has become fashionable in some circles to ridicule religion, the heart of man still hungers for Divine sustenance.

I wonder if you remember the Associated Press story (about 1971, it was) telling of a Johns Hopkins University medical researcher who discovered that the number of those suffering with fatal heart disease was twice as high for those who attend church infrequently, or not at all, as opposed to those who go to church at least once a week?

And I wonder how many of you heard about Stamford, Connecticut? A few years ago a custom started there—that of having church bells ring every Saturday evening from 6 to 6:15, pealing the message that "tomorrow is God's day, and we go to worship Him." I realize this movement is of special significance only to some segments of the spiritual community, but it's a healthy development, and what helps one group aids all those of differing religious persuasions.

The Stamford bell ringing started because an 81 year old grandmother was impressed with the fact that churches in Switzerland ring their bells every Saturday evening, and Switzerland has fought no wars in over 400 years.

Is it possible that we can bring our spiritual fires into full blaze again, or will they remain, like the Ark on Ararat, buried under the glacier of neglect?

Credits

Produced by Stanley L. Cahn
Edited by Harold A. Williams
Designed by Mossman Art Studio
Typography by Modern Linotypers, Inc.
Printed by Universal Lithographers, Inc.

About the author . . .

Don Spatz, a native of Reading, Pa., has a varied background as a writer, lecturer, music critic, columnist, teacher, public relations executive, and for the past decade or more, radio commentatator in the Maryland area.

Widely traveled, Mr. Spatz has roamed the world, exercising his skill as a photographer and speaker, combining them in years of activity as a travel lecturer.

Early in his career, he wrote hundreds of radio dramas, starring such artistic talent as Maurice Evans, Judith Anderson, Ethel Barrymore and Tallulah Bankhead. He also has numerous mystery and detective novels to his credit.

"Make This a Good Today," Mr. Spatz's first book of essays based on his radio shows, has proved very popular. At the request of many readers and listeners, he decided to develop this volume, with the added facet of Aubrey Bodine's illustrations.

About the photographer . . .

A. Aubrey Bodine was an imaginative photographer-historian who for almost 50 years used light on film as a painter uses brush on canvas. His resulting work was of such beauty and sensitivity that it made him known all over the world.

In his job as photographic director of the Baltimore Sunday Sun Magazine, he became a meticulous historian as well as photographer.

A competent and tireless craftsman, Mr. Bodine willingly waited for hours and even days in order to capture the desired mood or effect of a single composition. His visual essays of Maryland, Virginia and the Chesapeake Bay region earned Mr. Bodine international fame. He was the first American to have a one-man show in Russia.

His photo-documentary books have enjoyed unusual success. They are "The Face of Maryland", "Chesapeake Bay and Tidewater" and "The Face of Virginia". His pictures have been used as historic illustrations in scores of other books.

Upon his death in October, 1970, one of his colleagues on The Sun wrote: "If every man is mortal, it is none the less also true that the negatives and prints of a great photographer will be preserved, and studied and valued, long beyond his own life span."

OTHER BODINE PUBLICATIONS
OF BEAUTY AND SUBSTANCE

The Face of Maryland
by A. Aubrey Bodine. "The finest photodocumentary ever done of a beautiful State." Over 250 pictures/$22.50

Chesapeake Bay and Tidewater
by Mr. Bodine. A graphic pictorial story of the world's greatest bay. A classic. Over 250 pictures/$22.50

The Face of Virginia
by Mr. Bodine and Virginus Dabney. The Old Dominion handsomely portrayed in a magnificent photodocumentary . . . 335 pictures/$22.50

Maryland, A Picture History (1632-1976)
by Carleton Jones. Nearly 500 pictures of the Old Line state, laced with brief incisive commentary/$19.95

Bodine's Baltimore
by Mr. Bodine and Wilbur H. Hunter. A panorama of Baltimore's life style from 1924 to 1970 . . . a nostalgic record . . . 300 pictures/$14.95

Bodine—a Legend in His Time
by Harold A. Williams. A fascinating portrait of the uncommon, dedicated art photographer; 100 of his best pictures/$12.50

Baltimore, A Picture History
by Francis F. Bierne. More than 400 pictures of Baltimore, from the founding, with a charming commentary/$7.50

The Fells Point Story
by Norman G. Rukert. Baltimore's Fells Point has a stirring history, told here by a veteran of the scene/$8.95

The Neighborhood
by Gilbert Sandler with photographs by Mr. Bodine and drawings by Jacob Glushakow. An informal look at the enduring community of Little Italy in Baltimore. Cloth: $5.95; paper: $3.95

Bodine & Associates, Inc.
Fine books since 1952
1101 St. Paul Street, Baltimore, Md. 21202